TA and Training

TA and Training

The theory and use of transactional analysis in organisations

DAVE BARKER

Gower

Published by Gower Press, Teakfield Limited

Reprinted 1982 by Gower Publishing Company Limited,
Croft Road, Aldershot, Hants, GU11 3HR, England

British Library Cataloguing in Publication Data

Barker, Dave
TA and training.
1. Employees, Training of
2. Transactional analysis
I. Title
658.31'24 HF5549.5.T7

ISBN 0-566-02118-8

Typeset by Inforum Ltd., Portsmouth
Printed and bound in Great Britain
at The Pitman Press, Bath

Contents

Preface

My aim in writing this book has been two-fold. First to share with fellow professionals my experiences in and my enthusiasm for transactional analysis (TA). TA has emerged over the last decade from its confines as an alternative approach to therapy, for application within a relatively narrow section of society, to a wider acceptance and application with a broader public, namely those in full-time employment in a whole range of organisations. During the last four years I have been deeply involved in and committed to this development. My commitment is based on a personal belief that TA has a significant contribution to make in improving the effectiveness and satisfaction of relationships at work, the health of organisations and the abilities of managers, supervisors and indeed all employees to cope with changing social conditions.

My second aim has been to help fill a gap in the range of books on the subject. There are many based in the original setting of TA, but unfortunately many trainers are put off by TA therapy books, and their organisations even more so. There are some designed for use by managers, but with the exception of Carby and Thakur's *Transactional Analysis at Work* there is little available for trainers and associated professionals. This book has been written with such people in mind.

The text comprises a basic introduction to the theory (Chapters 1–10) and an overview of its application, including a number of pertinent training situations (Chapters 11–19). As far as the theory chapters are concerned, the material is by no means all-inclusive. Not only does the subject extend further and deeper than presented here but also lack of space prevents the consideration of such areas as miniscript theory and Berne's view of groups. However, the theory is, I hope, more than enough to begin with. The chapters on applications do not give detail on all the possible areas of use for TA, but (with a few exceptions) cover those that I can describe from first-hand experience as a trainer. The training programmes referred to also vary in the extent of the contribution from TA. I would like to make special mention of Chapter 10, 'TA and other approaches to psychology' (something of a philosopher's interlude); Chapter 11, 'The goals of TA and its application in training' (linking aims of TA to its application in training); and Chapter 19, 'Evaluation, limits and benefits'.

Throughout the writing of the book and after its completion I have had recurring thoughts on what could be changed, better presented, removed, added and so on. Consequently, in the manner of a request to the reader (and also in the best training tradition) I welcome any constructive feedback that anyone cares to share with me.

In the process of writing this book, many people have supported and encouraged me with their time, ideas and work, both directly and indirectly. First and foremost, I am deeply grateful to my wife, Tina, whose help was fundamental to carrying out the task in the first place. My thanks also go to Margaret Turpin, my supervisor in my studies for Special Fields Membership of the International Transactional Analysis Association. She helped me not only by encouraging my growth and learning in TA, but also by supporting me in taking a break from those studies whilst writing this book. My thanks also to all those clients and participants on training courses and workshops where I have introduced and used TA. Their willingness to receive, experience and explore TA for themselves makes the chapters on application possible.

I am indebted to John Giles, Director, and Robin Evenden, Deputy Director, of Roffey Park Management College for giving me time and resources for completing the book, and also to the secretaries at the College for their patience and hard work during the arduous task of typing these chapters.

As far as direct contributions are concerned, I am particularly thankful to my colleagues, Keri Phillips, for the time he spent formulating, adding to and checking various parts of the book and Neil Clark, for his help in compiling the index and checking the proofs. I am also grateful to Tony Fraser, Ben Bennett and David Roberts (all from the college) for their ideas and contributions; and, from outside the college, to Ron Clements for the material on TA in selling (Chapter 18), Mike Wellin for the work on TA and team building (the last section of Chapter 15) and Gordon Elliott for Figure 11.1. Finally my thanks go to all those, too numerous to mention, who have contributed to my learning and development, both in TA specifically and training generally.

Dave Barker

Acknowledgements

Acknowledgement is gratefully made for permission to reproduce the following material:

Dr Stephen Karpman for the use of his 'Drama Triangle' concept (pages 51–52)

Dr Ted Novey for the material on 'Middle-escence' (pages 205–207) and for the model for the 'Client-Consultant Relationship' (figure 15.1)

Dr S. Woollams, Dr M. Brown and Ms K. Huige for the use of material on 'Positive and Negative Aspects of Ego States' (pages 14–15) and 'Permissions' (pages 67–69)

Dr F.H. Ernst Junior for the use of his concept 'Life Positions' (see page 37)

Dr J.M. Dusay for the use of his concept 'Egograms' (pages 16–18)

Dr C. Steiner for the use of his concepts 'Stroke Economy' (pages 25–26), 'Script Matrix' (pages 65–67) and 'No Love, No Joy, No Mind' scripts (page 70)

Ms P. Levin for her ideas on Ego States and Child Development (see page 19)

Addison-Wesley, Reading, Mass., for permission to reproduce in modified form the 'Ego State Reaction Quiz' from 'Winning with People' by Dorothy Jongeward and Muriel James, copyright 1973 (see page 138) and also a summary of the chapter on the 'TACT programme' from 'Everybody Wins' by Dorothy Jongeward, copyright 1973 (see pages 210–211)

The Institute of Personnel Management for the material on 'Social Competence' from 'Transactional Analysis at Work' by K. Carby and M. Thakur, copyright 1976 (pages 92–94). Used with permission of the Institute of Personnel Management.

Ken Nixon for material from his article 'Customer Contact Skills: an assessment of alternative approaches' which appeared in *Industrial and Commercial Training*, Vol. 6, no. 1, January 1974 (see pages 92–94).

Part I
Understanding Transactional Analysis (TA)

1 Origins and history

This opening chapter outlines the origins and history of transactional analysis (TA). It will thus provide a useful context to the main concern of the book, i.e. the theory and practice of TA in organisations.

Any book on transactional analysis is destined to start with Eric Berne, the man and his work. Although there have been major contributions to TA theory and practice from other people who will be mentioned during the course of this book, Berne was undoubtedly the originator and first custodian. Since his death in 1970 there has been the growth of some mystique around him, which happens to many significant figures in all spheres of learning. For one person to be central to the development of a new domain of knowledge is not at all unusual, and his insights and ideas could well be as important a development for society as, say, Freud's or Einstein's half a century earlier.

Berne was born in Canada, but later became a naturalised American. His father was a doctor and Berne himself became a psychiatrist. During his early professional years (the 1940s and 1950s) various events and experiences were important to the developments he made, and the practices of TA today. First, he was influenced by establishment psychiatry and psychoanalysis. However, he disagreed with the orthodox practice of the day in terms of the elaborate language used, incomprehensible to the layman, and the 'expert–impersonal object' relationship between doctor and patient, where the therapist discusses a client's case in his absence. The outcome of this disagreement is the development in TA of a relatively simple, high-impact language to describe concepts and experiences that can be more readily shared with the layman as an equal. In addition, the language can be taught to clients, and they and the therapist or trainer can discuss their problems, experiences and choices using the shared language, in a two-person or group situation. These points are crucially important to the growing use of TA in organisational training and development; this is in direct opposition to Freudian psychoanalysis, for example, which has gained only limited acceptance as an intervention into organisations, as compared with its use in therapy.

At one time, Berne was under the guidance of Paul Federn, who was the first to coin the phrase 'ego states'.[1] One of the ego states, the 'Child', emerged as a consequence of Berne's wartime experiences.

Berne was a psychiatrist in the American army, involved in the task of interviewing many soldiers in a short time on their demobilisation. In order to cope with this situation he explored the use of intuition, a much faster way of perceiving than any deliberate, systematic, interviewing technique. This led to the notion of the Child as the source of intuition, amongst other things.

The concept of ego states gained further impetus from the famous 'cowpoke' story.[2] In this story, a client of Berne's, a lawyer by profession, commented on how he sometimes felt just like a little boy, not a professional man. (To illustrate this, the lawyer told a tale concerning an eight-year-old boy in a cowboy suit who was addressed as a 'cowpoke' by a grown-up, but responded that he wasn't really a cowpoke, just a little boy.) This alerted Berne to look for separate sets of ego states, first the Child and the Adult, and later the Parent.

In 1958 Berne established the San Francisco Social Psychiatry Seminars consisting of regular meetings with like-minded friends for the development of TA ideas. The use of the term '*social* psychiatry' is interesting. TA is both a theory of personality and also a theory of communication, paying considerable attention to what happens between people, unlike psychoanalysis. This communication theory aspect is another crucial factor in its use in organisations. Berne initially saw TA not as an alternative to the other forms of therapy, but as a preliminary or adjunct to help sort relationships out, before more penetrating intrapsychic work. Nowadays, TA is used for the latter, as for example the work of the Schiffs with schizophrenics.[3] In due course the San Francisco seminars gave rise to the International Transactional Analysis Association (ITAA), now the formal organising body for TA worldwide, with the aim of promoting the growth and development of TA, through conferences, publications and training.

The idea of ego states came to fruition in the early 1950s and the years that followed up to the 1970s saw the development of the other three key ideas in TA, i.e. transactions, games and scripts. Now it appears that most of the theoretical work is in terms of either 'picture straightening' or integrating and relating TA to other approaches.

Another important event in the history of TA was the publication of Berne's *Games People Play*[4] in 1964 in the USA and 1966 in the UK. This was the first TA book to gain wide public interest. The book indicates the possibility that TA offers not only a novel approach to therapy, but also a valid approach to personal growth and change and improving interpersonal communications in a wide variety of situations–social services, community development, racial and sexual equality, families and childrearing, educational, rehabilitation, organisations and business.

The particular focus of the present book is the use of TA in manufacturing, commercial and service sectors of industrial organisations and government agencies. While *Games People Play* opened the way for the use of TA more widely, it wasn't until the publication of *Everybody Wins*[5] in 1973 that the first use of TA in organisations was described in a book. One chapter detailed the use of TA in American Airlines and, not surprisingly, one of the first major applications of TA on this side of the Atlantic was in Aer Lingus. The October 1975 edition of the *Transactional Analysis Journal* (the official journal of the ITAA) was totally devoted to organisational applications. Since then, TA has been increasingly used in not only American, but also British industry. At the same time the 1970s have seen the establishment of a British Institute of Transactional Analysis as a focal point for the development of TA in the UK, and a steady growth in TA courses, conferences and training activity of all kinds.

REFERENCES

1 P. Federn, *Ego Psychology and the Psychoses,* Basic Books, 1952.
2 P. McCormick, *Ego States: Parent, Adult and Child*, Transactional Publications, 1977.
3 J.L. Schiff et al., *Cathexis Reader: Transactional Analysis Treatment of Psychosis,* Harper and Row, 1975.
4 E. Berne, *Games People Play,* Grove Press Inc., 1964; Andre Deutsch, 1966; Penguin, 1968.
5 D. Jongeward et al., *Everybody Wins: Transactional Analysis Applied to Organisations,* Addison-Wesley, 1973.

2 Ego states, exclusion and contamination

DEFINITION OF EGO STATES

An ego state is defined as a consistent pattern of feelings and experiences relating to corresponding, consistent patterns of behaviour.[1] There are considered to be three basic ego states: Parent, Adult and Child. Initial capital letters are used to denote the fact that in TA the words 'Parent, Adult and Child' are used in a different way from normal.

THE PARENT EGO STATE

The Parent is that part of us that reflects life as it is *taught.* It is the collection of all the things we do that our parents and other authority figures did, whether supporting or critical, including slogans, values and beliefs. It is the part of us that (in relation to ourselves and other people):

sets limits
disciplines, judges and criticises
gives advice and guidance
protects and nurtures
keeps traditions
makes rules and regulations about how life should be (the do's, don'ts, always, nevers, shoulds, shouldn'ts, musts, ought to's, have to's, can'ts, goods, bads).

As we move from group to group, organisation to organisation and culture to culture, our values and beliefs, judgements about the world, and permissions we give ourselves and others change. This is, of course, a very personal matter based on early experiences and the situations we face in adulthood. Some people are very changeable in this respect, whereas others are very rigid in their 'rules for life'.

THE ADULT EGO STATE

The Adult is the part of us that reflects life as it is *thought* and works things out by looking at the facts, and then makes decisions. It is unemotional and is concerned with 'what fits' and what is most useful. 'Adult' does *not* mean mature. The Adult:

gathers data from the outside world and also from the inside (how the Child feels and what the Child wants, what the Parent says, and what the stored memories of past decisions have to say)
sorts out the best alternatives from this data and estimates probabilities
plans the steps in the decision-making process.

The Adult is sometimes referred to as the 'minicomputer' in each one of us. An important value often expressed in TA is putting the 'Adult into the executive', i.e. using our Adult ego state to review data and make decisions before responding to a given situation.

THE CHILD EGO STATE

The Child ego state is the:

centre of our feelings and energy
source of our creativity, curiosity and intuition
'site' of our early experiences including those ways we have chosen to get attention from, and get along with, authority figures.

It is frequently referred to as that part of us that reflects life as it is *felt.* It is the most important ego state in terms of its actual 'control' over our lives. For example, personal change is not usually considered as possible unless the energy in our Child is committed to the change, however much our Adult values and understands the benefits of the change. The Child ego state is usually viewed as being fixed by the time we are about six years old.

REPRESENTATION OF EGO STATES

The basic representation of ego states is given in Figure 2.1. This is referred to as both the first order functional diagram and the first order structural diagram. The use of the terms functional and structural relate to the idea that there is a distinction between the expression of the ego states (the dynamic aspects, what we 'see') and the underlying structure (what is 'there' that gives rise to what we see).

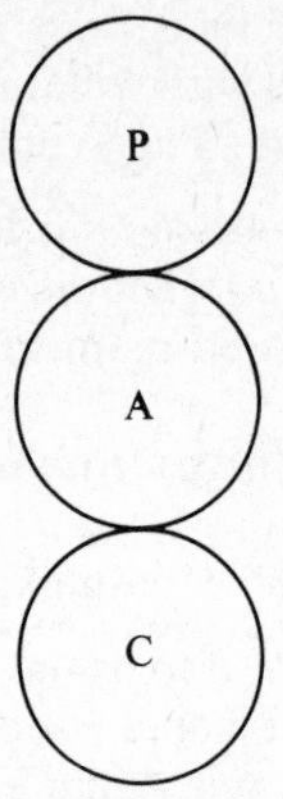

Figure 2.1 First order functional and first order structural diagram of the ego states

At the functional level the Parent and Child may each be further subdivided into two different facets or aspects, giving the second order functional diagram, Figure 2.2.

CRITICAL PARENT (CP)

The Critical Parent is that part of us that sets limits and makes judgements about ourselves and others. People are expressing their Critical Parent with statements like:
'Don't cross the road without looking both ways.'

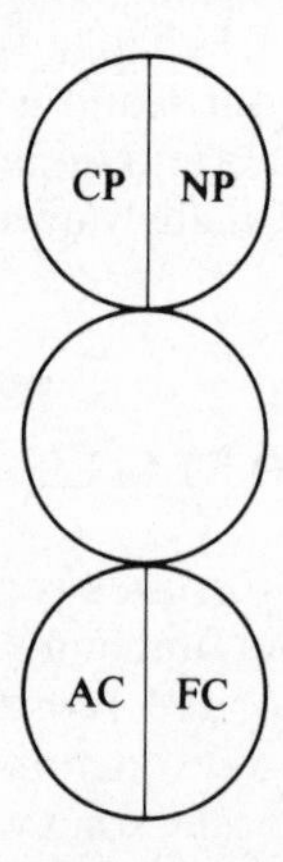

Figure 2.2 Second order functional diagram

'You shouldn't do that.'
'That was a bad mistake!'

NURTURING PARENT (NP)

This is the aspect of the Parent that gives permission and support to ourselves and others, and allows us to grow and develop. People are expressing their Nurturing Parent with statements like:
'Well done, that was a fine piece of work.'
'You have my wholehearted support in the matter!'

FREE OR NATURAL CHILD (FC OR NC)

This is the source of our spontaneity, energy and curiosity, with all our potential for life. It represents the way we are when we are born – natural, loving, carefree, adventurous and trusting – with all our capacities for leading a joyful and meaningful existence. This part of us knows no rules and consequently operates without regard for others and is unconcerned about their reactions. Witness the behaviour of the twelve-month-old exploring its environment! Of course, it would be impossible to maintain the structure of a society on such a basis, and without some adaptations.

In fact, in many grown-ups the adaptations are so extensive that they rarely use their Free Child. Some examples of the expression of the Free Child in an organisation are: the joy of a major breakthrough in research and the fun at an office party (alcohol first 'strips away' the Parent, then the Adult!).

ADAPTED CHILD

As suggested, it does not seem possible to live in a continuous Free Child state and live with other people at the same time. From an early age, we make adaptations to help us get along with and get attention from authority figures, most notably our own parents. Some of these may develop in line with general practice in our society, e.g. specific modes of eye and body contact;[2] saying 'please', 'thank you' and 'sorry' at the appropriate times; not making personal comments about others in public.

Note how uncomfortable we often feel with those who have not adapted to these culturally agreed ways of behaving. Many more adaptations are unique to the particular family and its situation, and are important in marking us out as individuals. Some examples that create problems in adulthood and are relevant to organisations are compliance, procrastination and rebellion.

Compliance

Some individuals learn when they are young that the way to get along is always to say 'yes'. Their problem in adulthood is saying 'yes' when their better judgement, experience and knowledge suggests that arguing the point and asserting themselves would be more appropriate. Some personal and organisational disasters might have been avoided if some people had not been so compliant in the past. (Of course, some people in power want nothing better than for others to do exactly what they are told!)

Procrastination

Some people learn when they are young that a good way to get attention is to procrastinate. Consider these examples from family life:

'C'mon, get a move on, or we'll miss the shops!'
'Look, put that doll down, tie your shoe laces up and let's get going. You're making us late again!'

If a child decides on this basis that delaying gets attention, in adulthood the individual may still be indulging in this behaviour. Certainly, being late is a good way to get attention in organisations (albeit negative) and it may use up more energy, money and time than it is worth (clock cards, counselling interviews, disciplinary interviews, etc.). Flexitime is no guarantee of cure.

Rebellion

Many children only get attention when they are 'naughty'. Such individuals in adulthood may continue this behaviour by seeking bosses and/or institutions (e.g. banks, local government, the police) to constantly fight and rebel against.

LITTLE PROFESSOR

Another functional aspect of the Child ego state is frequently introduced and used, although its relationship to the other two is unclear. This is the Little Professor, the intuitive part of us that senses things about other people in a flash. This part of us has those brilliant, non-logical insights giving us solutions to problems that typify some of the major breakthroughs in the growth of scientific knowledge.

At the structural level, the Parent and the Child are again subdivided, giving rise to the second order structural diagram (Figure 2.3).

For most purposes, the second order functional diagram (Figure 2.2) is the important one for organisational use and forms the basis for most of the work in this book. However, the second order structural diagram (Figure 2.3) is presented here for the sake of completion and also because the second order structural analysis of the Child will be referred to again in Chapter 9. At this stage, some important points are worth noting. First, the second order structural representation of the Child (Figure 2.3) shows a marked similarity to the second order functional aspects to which they give rise. Certainly A_1 is frequently equated with the 'Little Professor'. Second, the second order structural representation of the Parent is the internalised recordings of how parents and other authority figures have behaved directly to or in front of the individual. As a consequence, apparently childish behaviour may not necessarily be from C_2 but can be from the Child in the Parent, based directly on the behaviour of a person's mother or father.

DIAGNOSIS OF EGO STATES

Having elaborated the ego states and their various facets, including second order structure, the next question is how do we know what ego state we are in? There are four ways of identifying ego states – behavioural, social, historical and phenomenological. Of the four, the first two are the most useful to training in organisations.

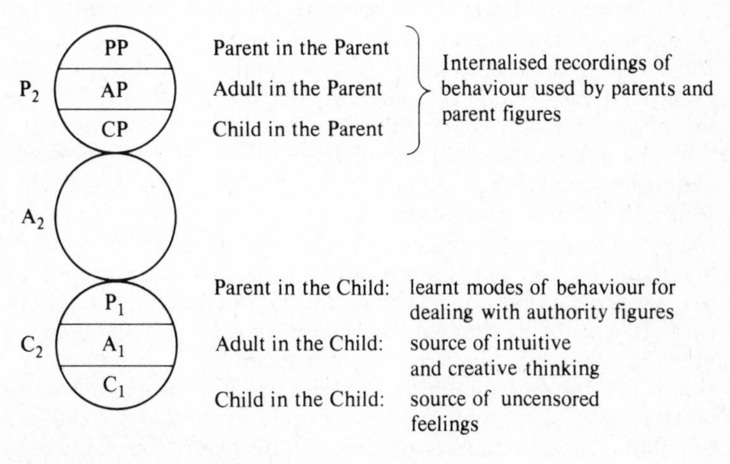

Figure 2.3 Second order structural diagram

BEHAVIOURAL

From a teaching and observation viewpoint this is the most important. Suppose a person says: 'You should get down to that job. I sympathise with your feelings of being overworked, but there is a lot to do.' They are behaving first in:

Critical Parent ('you should . . .') then in,
Nurturing Parent (' . . . I sympathise . . .') then in,
Adult (' . . . there is a lot to do.').

If this is followed with, 'I've got a great idea, let's have a departmental party when this rush is over! Hang on though, I'm worried what the MD would think of that', the same person is starting in

Free Child ('I've got a great idea . . .') and then ending in,
Adapted Child (' . . . hang on though I'm worried . . .').

In other words, the words and phrases used are indicative of the ego state that person is in, together with the way the words and phrases are spoken, and the body language (or 'non-verbals') and general attitude accompanying the words. It may not be possible to be accurate in this diagnosis of self or others all the time, in particular of oneself. However, it gives us a starting point and at least an opportunity to make more appropriate and effective choices in our interpersonal relationships by identifying where we and others are in ego-state terms. Figure 2.4 shows some typical behaviours for the different ego states.

The words used are not necessarily the most important clue to a person's ego state. While some phrases are more likely to come from one ego state than any other (e.g. 'you should . . .' is almost invariably Critical Parent), others vary; after all, there are many different ways to say 'good morning', each with a different message. Consider the question, 'How long did it take you, Jones?' said in an even clear calm enquiring voice (Adult), compared with 'How long did it take *you*, Jones?' said in a loud voice with a stress on '*you*', a frown on the speaker's face and a pointed finger aimed at Jones. These examples highlight the fact that it's not what we say, but how (tones, body language, etc.) that affects the quality of our relationships so drastically. It is probable that words account for only a small percentage of the 'messages' we give to others in face-to-face situations, a view supported by the sometimes inadequate and misleading nature of written communication (memos, letters, reports, etc.) and even of telephone conversations (which may convey voice tones, but not body

Figure 2.4. Some behavioural aspects of ego states

Ego state	*Typical words/phrases*	*Typical voice tone*	*Typical behaviour*	*Typical attitudes*
Critical Parent	'That's disgraceful'	sneering	furrowed brow	moralistic
	'You ought'	angry	pointed finger	judgemental
	'You must always'	condescending	scowling face	
	'Don't ask questions'	critical	set jaw	authoritarian
	'Because I said so'	disgusted	pounding on table	
Nurturing Parent	'Well done young man!'	sympathetic	pat on the back	caring
	'Splendid!'	warm	consoling touch	permissive
	'What a lovely boy!'	encouraging	benevolent smile	supportive
	'Don't worry'			understanding
	'I'll sort it out for you'			
Adult	'How?'	clear	relaxed	non-judgemental
	'When?'	calm	attentive and aware	open-minded
	'Where?'	enquiring	level eye contact	interested
	'Let's look at it again'			confident
	'It's 6.30'			
Adapted Child	'I'll try hard'	whiny	downcast eyes	compliant
	'Please can I?'	placating	vigorous head nodding	defiant
	'I can't'	mumbling	nail biting	delaying
	'Please'	taunting	slumped and dejected posture	passive
	'Thank you'		spitefulness	complaining
Free Child	'I want'	loud	laughing with someone	curious
	'Wow!'	fast	noisy crying	energetic
	'I feel great'		demonstration of feelings	fun-loving
			constantly changing behaviour	spontaneous

language). In diagnosing ego states in others it is important to take note of not only words, but also voice tones, gestures, postures and facial expressions.

SOCIAL

If in response to someone else's comment I instantaneously feel crest-fallen, guilty or uncomfortable, the chances are that the other person has used their Critical Parent and I have responded from my Adapted Child. In other words it is possible to diagnose the ego state of the other person from our own responses following the social exchanges between us. If a manager constantly feels like criticising, admonishing and 'kicking' a particular subordinate, the possibility is that the latter spends much time in Adapted Child when the two of them are together.

HISTORICAL

A participant on a TA-based human relations course once reported that sometimes he 'observed' himself sitting in a chair just as his father did. At this point he was almost certainly in his Parent ego state, as is any observation that 'I' am behaving just as a parent or other authority figure did in the past. Similarly a recollection such as 'Right now I feel just as I did in the distant past when I was a six-year old' is an indicator of being in the Child. These are examples of historical diagnosis.

PHENOMENOLOGICAL

This occurs when an individual reflects on his own feelings, thoughts and behaviour and determines whether he is in Parent, Adult or Child. This kind of experience may be supported by the use of various training or therapy techniques.

POSITIVE AND NEGATIVE ASPECTS OF EGO STATES [3]

No one ego state is either good or bad. Behaviour from each ego state may be 'positive' or 'negative' in the sense of having healthy, helpful and effective outcomes for relationship and work, or the opposite, depending on the situation. Some examples of this are shown in Figure 2.5.

Figure 2.5 Positive and negative aspects of ego states

Positive Nurturing Parent
Cares for another person when they need or want it

Negative Nurturing Parent
Does things for others when not needed and not requested (e.g. 'Let me do it for you')

Positive Critical Parent
Stands up for own rights without putting others down or sets limits that safeguard others (e.g. 'You must look both ways before crossing the road')

Negative Critical Parent
Takes away the self-worth of another person (e.g. 'You're no good')

Positive Adapted Child
Will use automatic behaviour in line with social custom (e.g. use of 'please', 'thank you', 'sorry' at the appropriate times)

Negative Adapted Child
Use of self-destructive behaviour to get attention from others (e.g. persistent lateness). Constant delaying, compliance and rebellion are typical negative adaptations

Positive Free Child
Expresses directly what's on his/her mind, has fun and does not hurt anyone

Negative Free Child
May hurt self or others while having fun

It does seem that some people have an over-reliance on one or more of their ego states in preference to others. For example, a boss who spends a lot of his time in Critical Parent may create all kinds of difficulties for his staff. One goal of TA is to help people attain access to behaviours from all the ego states so that they have maximum choices in dealing with others. Part of this goal, referred to earlier, is 'putting the Adult in the executive', i.e. thinking before responding to others, rather than responding instantaneously to others on every occasion, from Parent or Adapted Child. Some people have misinterpreted this to imply that the Adult is the most 'desirable' ego state; this is not so.

EGO STATES AND CULTURE

The typical behaviours displayed in the Parent and Adapted Child ego states will vary significantly from country to country, and culture to culture, in addition to the idiosyncratic variations from individual to individual and family to family. For example, what are learnt, unthinking Adapted Child behaviours in one country may be totally alien to a visitor or immigrant from another country and demand his/her modifying behaviour to cope with this. It does seem, however, that the basic model of ego states transfers quite readily from one culture to another, as witnessed by the international use of TA.

INTERNAL DIALOGUE

In any individual, the ego states do not operate independently of each other, and frequently interact to give an 'internal dialogue'.[4] A manager sitting at home thinking about a work situation may have a Critical Parent–Adapted Child internal dialogue resulting in a depressed attitude – which may be all his/her spouse or colleagues notice. This is represented in Fig. 2.6. His or her own Parent is giving his or her Child a lot of trouble. If the dialogue continues, it may get in the way of work, and job performance may begin to suffer. When operating internally in this way, the Parent ego state is referred to as the 'influencing Parent'.[5] As suggested, it is not so easy for others to spot this behaviour, unlike Parent behaviour aimed externally, referred to as the active Parent. The active and influencing Parents may be very different in their Critical and Nurturing qualities, so that someone may be very helpful and supportive to others, but tough on themselves (e.g. working themselves to death).

The internal dialogue can absorb a great deal of energy, often to no avail, unless an educated Adult ego state monitors and blocks the out-of-date oppression of the Parent and misconceptions of the Child.

EGOGRAMS

The relative extents to which different individuals behave in ego state terms in different situations can be portrayed diagramatically as in Figure 2.7.

Alternatively this idea can be portrayed as a histogram referred to in TA as an *egogram*.[6] For example, manager X in Figure 2.7 would be given the egogram shown in Figure 2.8. In this manner, the behaviour of manager X is given a semiquantitative breakdown, according to any

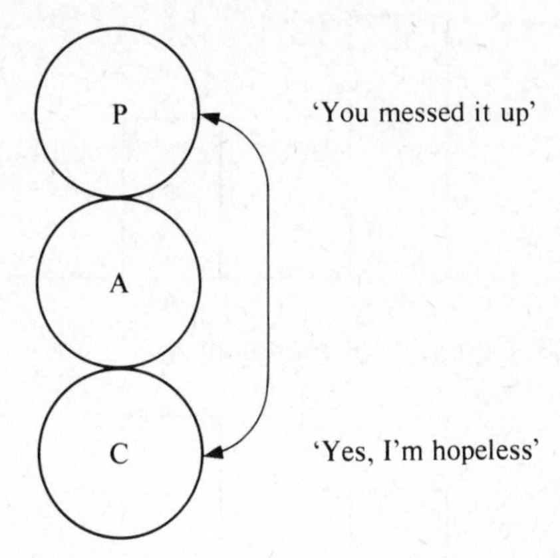

Figure 2.6 Internal dialogue

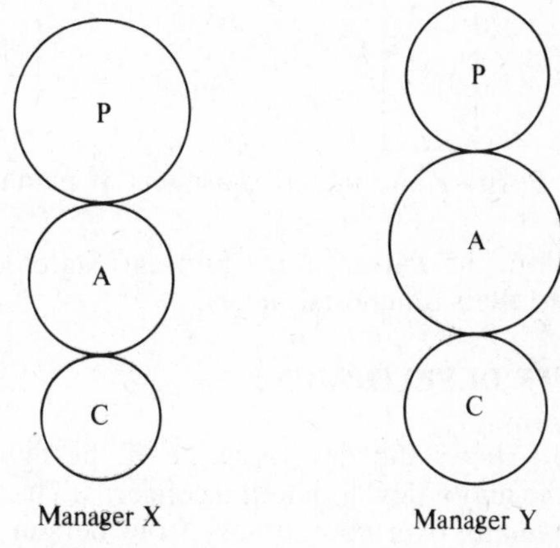

Figure 2.7 The behaviour of different managers portrayed in ego-state terms

given situation. For example:

how he sees himself on the course and how others see him on the course
how others see him on day 2 of the course and how others see him on day 5 of the course
how he sees himself at work and how he sees himself at home.

Hence we have a simple but effective analytical and feedback tool for use in training situations. A further variation is to consider the positive and negative aspects, as in Figure 2.9.

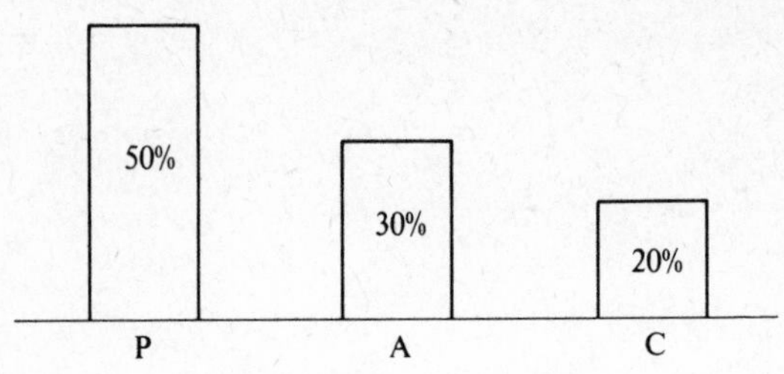

Figure 2.8 Egogram of manager X

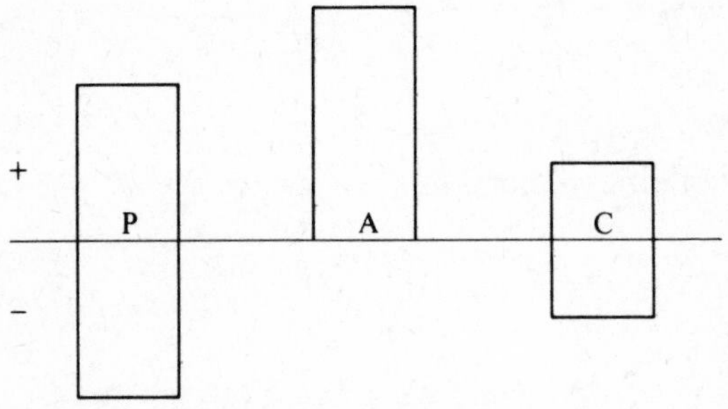

Figure 2.9 Positive and negative aspects of manager X's egogram

In addition, the Parent and Child ego states can be further subdivided into their functional facets.

EGO-STATE DEVELOPMENT

Figure 2.10 shows the development of the ego states from birth, including the major developmental concerns. The time periods quoted are approximate, overlap and vary from person to person. Furthermore, they may be disturbed by problems of upbringing, environment or genetics. Developmental activities that are not completed during the first ten years of life are 'recycled' during adolescence (widely recognised as a 'difficult' time). This recycling may occur again around the ages of 35 to 45 years, referred to as 'middle-escence'. This period is often associated with career difficulties and decline in work performance among managers. (The problem of middle-escence is discussed further in Chapter 18.)

EXCLUSION

Exclusion is the reliance on one ego state under all but the most favourable circumstances, without recourse to behaviour from the

Figure 2.10 Development of ego states[7]

Age	*Structural ego state*	*Functional ego state*	*Major concerns*
0–6 months	C_1	Natural Child	Feeding and stroking Getting immediate response to crying Dependency and helplessness Importance of our existence
6–18 months	A_1	Little Professor	Exploration Development of curiosity, creativity, motivation and 'tricks' to get attention from authority figures
18 months – 3 years	A_2	Adult	Separation Development of thinking Control, with development of compliance or rebellion
3–6 years	P_1	Adapted Child	Development and exercise of imagination Development of personal power Deciding what kind of person we are, and what kind of life we will lead
7–10 years	P_2	Parent	Creative activity Disagreeing and arguing Establishing values

other two. The outward signs of exclusion are predictable attitudes and behaviours whatever the situation, with no flexibility. A person with a high level of exclusion always seems to act and respond in a certain way, particularly under threat or pressure. In terms of behaviour, an individual may appear to others as a Constant Parent, Constant Adult or Constant Child.

THE CONSTANT PARENT

The Constant Parent excludes Adult and Child for most of the time. In terms of their managerial behaviour, such a person is likely to be controlling, judgemental and authoritarian (Critical Parent) towards others and/or 'smothering' and overcaring (Nurturing Parent). Their subordinates are likely to experience themselves as having no power, nor opportunities to develop their problem-solving and decision-making skills.

THE CONSTANT ADULT

The Constant Adult excludes Parent and Child for most of the time. Such an individual is likely to be a very effective thinker, planner and technical problem-solver. However, he/she will be experienced by colleagues as being humourless (since devoid of the fun, charm and spontaneity of the Child) and also uncommitted in debates about rights and wrongs (since devoid of values and standards of the Parent).

THE CONSTANT CHILD

The Constant Child excludes Parent and Adult for most of the time. Such a person is likely to be charming, humorous and creative, impulsive, perhaps immoral and certainly lacking skills in rational thinking (Adult) and well-defined social values (Parent).

People with exclusion are likely to create difficulties for others they work with in terms of their management style and interpersonal skills. They may not even be aware of these difficulties, unless they receive and 'digest' feedback. In many cases, the exclusion may be partial. For example, over-reliance on Critical Parent with little Nurturing Parent is common in managers, as is their exclusion of the Free Child (except perhaps when playing with children).

CONTAMINATION

Contamination is the intrusion of either the Parent and/or Child ego state into the Adult (Figure 2.11). The consequence of contamination is a disturbance of the problem-solving and decision-making capacity of the Adult. When the contaminated thinking is confronted (e.g. 'Come now, all women don't make bad managers') the response may be to defend the contamination even more strongly ('Yes, they definitely do'). Parent-contaminated Adult leads to prejudices, tenaciously held opinions not updated in the face of data from the outside world. These prejudices may be formed early in life from the influence of parent or other authority figures, or may be based on one single, vivid experience in adulthood. Prejudices abound in organisations; for example: sales departments in relation to production departments (and vice versa); managers in relation to worker (and vice versa); and men in relation to women (and vice versa). They can act as a barrier to effective communication and joint problem-solving between individuals and groups, though there are some effective approaches for dealing with them.[8]

Child contamination of the Adult leads to delusions, which in their severe form require therapy. In work situations, delusions are likely to lead to impaired or reduced job performance. For example, the employee who 'feels' that he is not good enough to do the job. This 'feeling' may well be seen by him as fact, although his colleagues and boss may have different facts about his effectiveness. Managers under high work stress sometimes develop delusions, as do work groups presented with rumours and partial information concerning restructuring and redundancies.

IMPLICATIONS FOR ORGANISATIONS AND TRAINERS

The analysis of ego states may well be a process of making explicit the implicit, but there are a whole number of implications and choices for

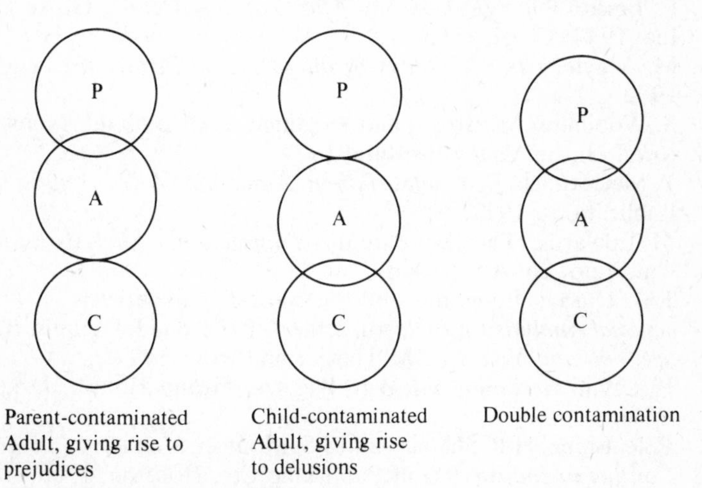

Figure 2.11 Contamination

organisations based on the concept. It presents a way of classifying and understanding the vagaries of individuals' behaviour in a penetrating way without necessarily moving into the realms of clinical psychology. It serves as a reminder that people's behaviour inside and outside work is related not only to the situation, but also to their own history and experience. Probably the majority of organisations in Western society require creativity for survival in a changing world, which in turn implies creating situations where people can respond and behave from Adult and Free Child. This may mean in many cases the reduction of Parent behaviour by authority figures. The potential benefit is a reduction in 'grudging' compliance from the Adapted Child of employees and an increase in the more creative and energetic motivation of the Free Child.

The implications of TA for trainers are a major theme of this book. Certainly as both a philosophy and as a tool for their use, it presents management trainers, management and organisational development advisers and the personnel profession generally with directions for organisations to develop if they are to remain viable and successful. However, TA has its uses in other, more specific areas of training. For example, those responsible for apprentice training can use the concept of ego states for the guidance and development of those under their charge.

REFERENCES

1 E. Berne, *What Do You Say After You Say Hello?*, Grove Press Inc. 1972; Corgi, 1975.
2 M. Argyle, *The Psychology of Interpersonal Behaviour,* Penguin, 1972.
3 S. Woollams, M. Brown and K. Huige, *Transactional Analysis in Brief,* Huron Valley Institute, 1974.
4 P. McCormick, *Ego States: Parent, Adult and Child,* Transactional Publications, 1977.
5 M. Edwards, 'The Two Parents', *Transactional Analysis Bulletin,* vol. 7, no. 26, April 1966.
6 J.M. Dusay, 'Egograms and the constancy hypothesis' in *Transactional Analysis Journal,* vol. 2, no. 3, 1972; and *Egograms: How I See You and You See Me,* Harper and Row, 1977.
7 P. Levin, *Becoming the Way We Are,* Group House, Berkeley, 1974.
8 R.R. Blake, H.P. Shepard and J.S. Mouton, *Managing Intergroup Conflict in Industry,* Gulf Publishing Co., Houston, 1965.

3 Strokes

RENÉ SPITZ

Another important concept in TA is strokes. The development of the idea owes much to the work of René Spitz.[1] Spitz studied very young institutionalised children and observed a higher incidence of psychological damage, physical retardation and death rate from common infant diseases than normal. He related this to the lack of available sensory stimulation in institutions. Although there was adequate warmth, shelter, food and cleanliness, the absence of mother meant that there was a dearth of physical handling and other forms of contact and recognition. The exchange of physical and, later, non-physical forms of recognition thus appears to be an important part of human development and a central aspect of human needs.

Spitz's work and its implications led to the development of the concept of strokes, a concept that has received a good deal of attention in the use of TA in training and in therapy. A stroke is defined as any act implying recognition of another's presence, whether verbally, non-verbally (a frown or smile, for instance) or by physical contact.[2] As we grow up the emphasis changes (in Western cultures anyway) from exchanging physical strokes to exchanging verbal, as physical contact and stimulation become taboo except in prescribed situations.

STROKES

Strokes may conveniently be classified as shown in Figure 3.1. There is a fundamental assumption in TA that negative strokes are better than no strokes. In other words, when we are young we will seek negative recognition, rather than be ignored, because it at least indicates that we are alive. This gives an explanation of 'naughty' behaviour in children and has its parallels in grown-up behaviour (e.g. 'Ah well, when the boss is shouting at me, at least he's recognising I'm here'). Clearly the best strokes for healthy development and a fulfilling life are positive strokes for being. Functioning in society and maintaining effective relationships demand positive strokes for doing and sometimes negative strokes for doing. Negative strokes for being and no strokes seem undesirable and destructive from all points of view. The stroke classification is by no means discrete since some comments may combine elements of two (e.g. 'You're capable of much better than that'). Also, the classification of a stroke depends on what the receiver 'hears' as well as what the sender intends.

Figure 3.1 Classification of strokes

Type	*Example*
Positive for being (unconditional)	'You're great'
Positive for doing (conditional)	'If you achieve your targets, you'll get promotion'
Negative for doing (conditional)	'You've made such a mess, I'm not giving you another chance'
Negative for being (unconditional)	'I just don't like you'
No strokes	–

STROKE BALANCE AND STROKE RESERVOIR

Stroke balance refers to the types of strokes we experience when we are young and the effect of this later in life. For example, we may experience lots of negative strokes when we are young, (Figure 3.2). Alternatively our stroke balance may be the reverse, with lots of positive strokes. Either way the 'balance' we experience when we are young is 'familiar' and 'comfortable' to us, however positive or negative. An assumption is then made in TA that whatever balance we experience when we are young we seek to recreate in adulthood because of its familiarity and comfortableness. It may seem strange that people might spend their lives looking for a high percentage of negative strokes and yet some people do set themselves up to be 'kicked' with great regularity. Another experience that supports the notion of stroke balance is the 'how long can my good luck last?' sense that some people have. Sooner or later that good luck turns to bad – and that person makes sure it does.

Related to stroke balance is the idea of stroke reservoir or 'credit bank'.[3] For example, if we are low on positive strokes, we will in some way be 'uncomfortable' (unhappy or depressed) until we have taken some steps to refill the reservoir and redress the balance. One way we can do that is to remind ourselves of strokes received in the past.

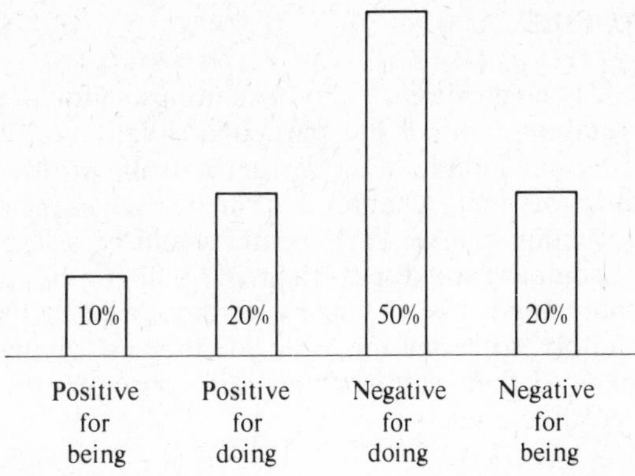

Figure 3.2 An individual stroke balance (in percentages)

STROKE ECONOMY[4]

The stroke economy consists of five basic rules, as follows:

1 Don't give positive strokes if you have them to give.
In other words, don't freely give of your good feelings towards others

2 Don't ask for positive strokes when you need them.
In other words, don't ask for comfort but wait for it to be given

3 Don't accept positive strokes.
Even if, deep down, you want to hear good things about yourself, reject the positive strokes you are offered

4 Don't reject strokes when you don't want them.
For example, women get strokes for beauty when an increasing number are interested in getting strokes for being intelligent or powerful and don't want to hear about their looks all the time

5 Don't give yourself strokes.
Our society puts a lot of pressure on people not to brag or otherwise share with others the good things about themselves.

The cultural message underlying these rules is that positive strokes are limited in supply, while negative strokes are abundant.

These stroke economy rules are messages carried around in people's heads in or out of awareness, and underscored by early Parent messages. Many people seem to carry one or more of them in some sizeable way, few of us being capable of a totally free exchange of strokes. The rules lead to a loveless life plan or script, referred to in Chapter 9.

STROKE PROFILE

A stroke profile is a pictorial way of representing an individual's choice of strokes in relation to others in a particular situation or time period. Figure 3.3 gives an example of a manager's stroke profile in his job. Rather like the egogram in Chapter 2, it can be used as the basis for an exercise in a training course. Participants would be asked to fill out these profiles, compare and discuss them in small groups and consider any changes they might like to make with those aspects that concern them. For example, someone might decide they are giving too many negative strokes to their subordinates and consequently change to giving more positive ones.

IMPLICATIONS FOR ORGANISATIONS AND TRAINING

This century has seen the development of automation and mass production and as a consequence the reduction in the stroke content inherent in many jobs. The growth of job enrichment in the 1960s and 1970s has been a reaction to this deskilling and an attempt to put

	Extent	*Receive*	*Give*	*Ask for*	*Refuse*
Positive strokes	Always				
	Usually				
	Sometimes				
	Almost never				
Negative strokes	Almost never				
	Sometimes				
	Usually				
	Always				

Figure 3.3 Stroke profile of a manager at work

positive strokes back into work. The last two decades have also seen attempts to democratise the workplace by improving relationships between employees at all levels. This has often involved changing the emphasis from the exchange of negative to the exchange of positive strokes. However, our emphasis on a competitive society tends to support the continued exchange of negative strokes as a means of maintaining that competition and progressing up the 'ladder of success' at the expense of others. All too often the only strokes available in organisations are negative ones. The principle of 'management by exception' often degenerates into, 'Don't bother me when things are going well, but watch out when things go wrong!' Organisations are often ideal locations for those with a negative stroke balance to fulfil their needs. For example, lateness is a great way to attract negative strokes, and managers devote large amounts of energy, time and money in dealing with it, as well as handing out countless negative strokes to the transgressors. Many people find switching to giving and receiving positive strokes uncomfortable at first, which is not surprising, after a lifetime of giving and receiving negative ones. However, organisations have everything to gain in making such a change, in terms of increased work effectiveness as well as improved relationships.

As far as trainers are concerned, many pay attention to the need for positive strokes in encouraging trainees to learn new skills, whether technical or social. They are sometimes the recipient of negative strokes, though – which may say something about their stroke balance.

REFERENCES

1 R. Spitz, 'Hospitalism, genesis of psychiatric conditions in early childhood', *Psychoanalytic Study of the Child,* vol. 1, 1945.
2 D. Kupfer, 'On "stroking" ', *Transactional Analysis Bulletin*, vol. 1, no. 2, 1962.
3 F. English, 'Strokes in the credit bank for David Kupfer', *Transactional Analysis Journal,* vol. 1, no. 3, 1971.
4 C.M. Steiner, *Scripts People Live,* Grove Press Inc., 1974; Bantam Books, 1975.

4 Transactions

While the term 'transactional analysis' is used to cover all the work originating from Eric Berne and his colleagues in the San Francisco Seminar, transactional analysis proper refers to the analysis of interactions between people.[1] A transaction is defined as *the unit of social intercourse,* consisting of a stimulus followed by a response, which may in turn become a stimulus for a further response, and so on. Each transaction, therefore, consists of two strokes, or units of recognition.

A STORY

Training officer Ted is new to his job, enthusiastic, hardworking, bright and developing too fast for his boss, training manager Tom. Ted handles the induction courses for the new recruits, including some presentations himself, as well as organising the other speakers. While doing a government sponsored training officers' course, Ted chose his work on induction courses as the subject matter for a mid-course project. He, and his course tutors, were particularly interested in the evaluation of induction, and Ted developed a number of useful questionnaires for this process. On completion of the project, Ted wrote up the project and presented it to the course tutors. The personnel director of Ted's organisation also requested a copy, which meant that Tom, the director's subordinate, was more than usually interested in seeing it, so Ted put a copy on his desk.

'Where's the induction project report?' said Tom

'On your desk', said Ted

So Tom duly studied it in his office. Two hours later he came out of his office.

'I think I've done a great report', said Ted enthusiastically

'Yes, you've done very well there, I'm very proud of you', said Tom patting Ted on the shoulder

Ted skipped off, full of the joys of life, to crow about his report to the secretaries and his colleagues in the personnel department. Soon he came back to Tom.

'Where's my report?' said Ted to Tom

'Can't you look for yourself!' retorted Tom. 'I put it back on your desk after you went out on your little boasting trip!'

Ted sidled guiltily over to his desk. Next day Ted came angrily into Tom's office.

'Those . . . in production, they've just cancelled two of their people on the next induction course', said Ted. 'What a damn nuisance they are!'

'Well, you should organise things more effectively', said Tom smugly.

Ted stopped dead in his tracks, paused and then left Tom's office confused.

Ted was interested in doing management training some day, thinking it was the most glamorous training to do. Tom had asked him to find a suitable training programme to develop his skill in this area, and thumbing through a management college prospectus, Ted had found the ideal course for introducing himself to management training. The next day he rushed excitedly into Tom's office.

'Heh, I've found just the right course for me. I want to go on it', said Ted

'Look, you should know better than to bother me right now', said Tom. 'It's the monthly personnel meeting tomorrow'

Ted backed off confused and disappointed. Half an hour later, he decided to go back into Tom's office and try his luck again.

'This course I mentioned to you, I think it's just the right one', said Ted. 'The *ABC* company sent two of their training officers on it'

'Did they? Well OK I'll book you on it straight away', said Tom, hurriedly.

Ted left feeling satisfied.

Several months later, Ted was improving all the time, even catching his boss up in terms of skill as a trainer. Tom was increasingly unhappy about this and thought Ted was getting too big for his boots and decided to have a 'chat' with him.

'Come into my office for a chat', said Tom brusquely.

'Yes, OK then', replied Ted nervously.

Six months later Ted got himself a job as a training manager in a firm six miles away.

TYPES OF TRANSACTIONS

We can use our opening story to illustrate the different types of transactions. Transactions are either simple or complex. A simple transaction involves the use of only one ego state by the initiator and one by the responder. A complex transaction involves the use of two ego states by either initiator or responder or both.

There are two kinds of simple transactions – crossed and complementary – and two kinds of complex transactions – angular and duplex.

COMPLEMENTARY TRANSACTION

In this simple transaction the ego state that is addressed is the one that responds. In addition the response is addressed to the ego state that initiated the transaction. From the previous story, the first exchange between Tom and Ted is an example as shown in Figure 4.1. In this first exchange between Tom and Ted, Tom asks a question from his Adult, addressing it to Ted's Adult. Ted responds with his Adult, returning his response to Tom's Adult, the initiating ego state.

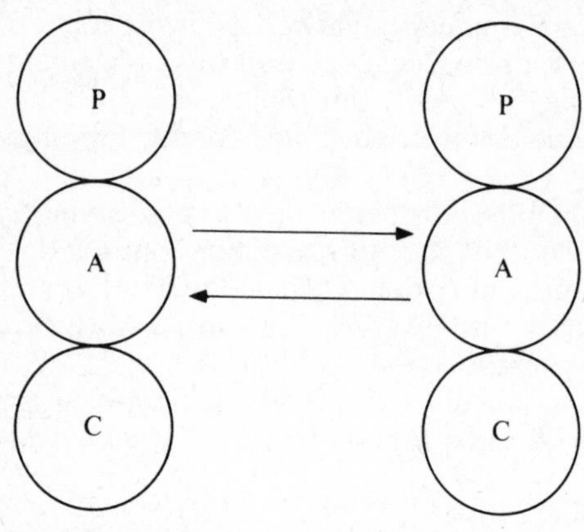

Tom: 'Where's the induction project report?' *Ted*: 'On your desk'

Figure 4.1 An Adult to Adult complementary transaction

There are nine possible complementary transactions as shown in Figure 4.2 and this number increases if we introduce the facets of the ego states (Critical Parent, Nurturing Parent, etc.).

The second exchange between Ted and Tom is a complementary

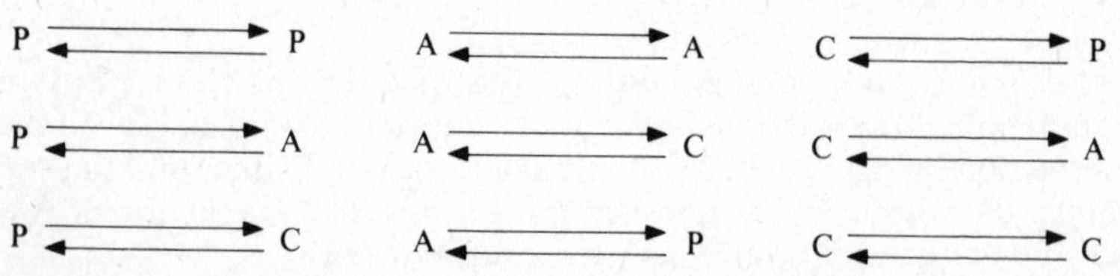

Figure 4.2 The possible complementary transactions

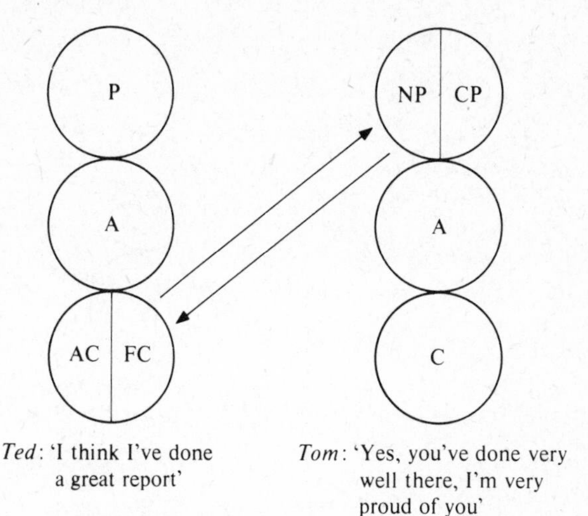

Figure 4.3 A Free Child to Nurturing Parent complementary transaction

transaction involving Ted's Free Child and Tom's Nurturing Parent, Figure 4.3.

CROSSED TRANSACTION

This is also a simple transaction, but one in which the ego state the respondent uses is either not the one addressed or, if it is the one addressed, it in turn does not address the initiating ego state. To illustrate this, the second, third and fourth quotes are examples, shown in Figure 4.4.

In Figure 4.4(i) Ted asks for information from Tom's Adult, but gets a response from Tom's (Critical) Parent instead, aimed at his (Adapted) Child. In Figure 4.4(ii) Ted is looking for a joint Parent–Parent complaining session about the production department. He hooks Tom's Parent well enough, but Tom's response is addressed to Ted's own (Adapted) Child. In Figure 4.4(iii), Ted attempts to engage Tom's Nurturing Parent from his excited Free Child, but gets thumped by Tom's Critical Parent instead.

The number of different kinds of crossed transactions that are theoretically possible is seventy-two, if we stay with first order ego state analysis (see Chapter 2) and much larger still if we use second order structural or functional analysis, hence highlighting the potential complexity of human relations. Four of the most common ones (certainly in organisations) are shown in Figure 4.5.

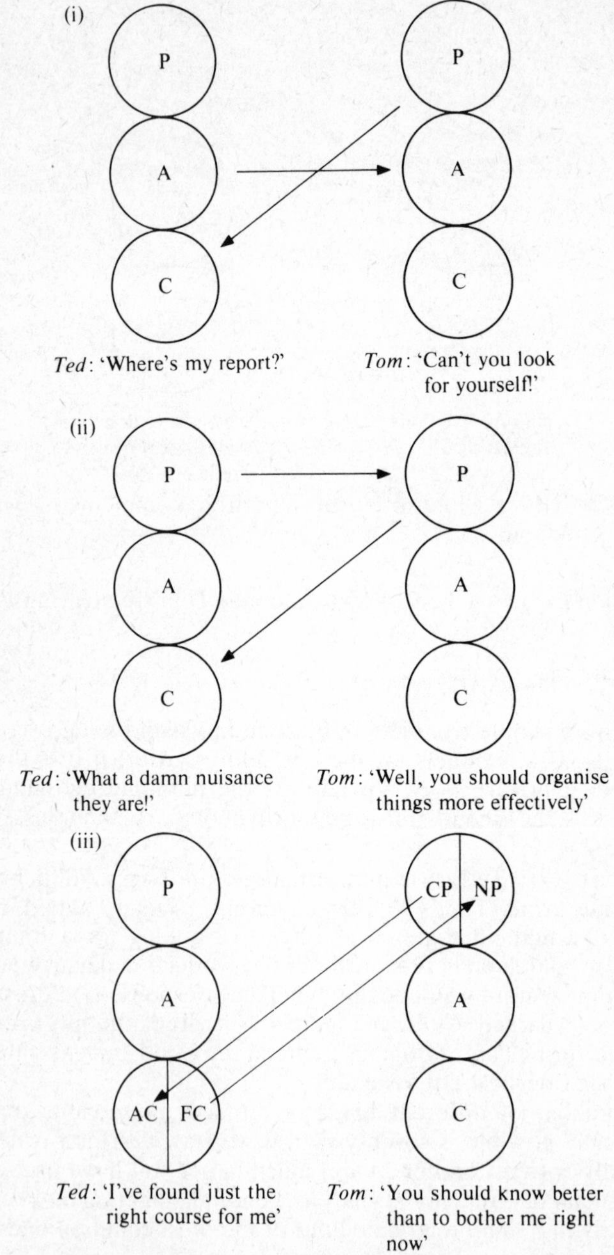

Figure 4.4 Three typical crossed transactions

Figure 4.5 Four common crossed transactions

Type	*Initiator*	*Responder*
(*a*)	A – A	C – P
(*b*)	A – A	P – C
(*c*)	C – P	A – A
(*d*)	P – C	A – A

An example of type (*b*) is shown in Figure 4.4(i). Examples of the other types are shown in the following transactions involving Ted and Tom:

'Have you finished the report yet?' asks Tom
'Oh Lord, I'm so busy at the moment', whines Ted [type (*a*)]

'I just don't know what to do with this course design', whines Ted
'Well, what are your choices as you see it?' asks Tom [type (*c*)]

'I've told you before to refer to the training records', thunders Tom
'I have done, but some of them aren't complete', says Ted [type (*d*)]

In everyday experience what distinguishes a crossed transaction from a complementary one is that it may cause the smooth flow of communication to break down, i.e. there is a 'hiccup' and often a pause while the initiator then considers which ego state to respond from. At first sight, the smooth flowing complementary transaction seems more supportive of good human relations than the 'jar' of crossed transactions. However, this all depends on the situation. A high frequency of P–C transactions between two adults may signal an oppressive relationship and crossed transactions may be a better choice for those who do not wish to be abused or continuously put down.

ANGULAR TRANSACTION

In this complex transaction, two messages are sent simultaneously from the ego state of one individual to another. The two messages comprise a spoken social one received by one ego state of the recipient and an unspoken psychological or ulterior one received by another ego state of the recipient. In our story, the sixth exchange is an example of an angular transaction as shown in Figure 4.6.

Ted's social message is apparently Adult to Adult but at an ulterior level he is aiming to hook the competitive aspect of Tom's Child that doesn't want to be one down to a rival organisation. Ted succeeds in this, Tom responding from his Child (I'll book you on it straight away').

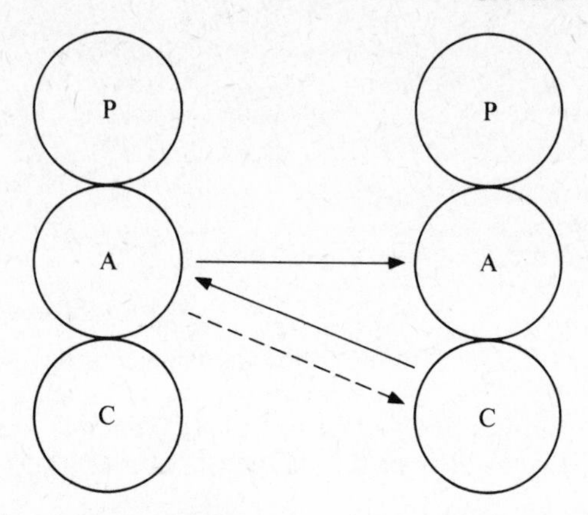

Ted: 'The ABC company sent two of their training officers on it' (*social message*) 'You can't afford to be one down to them' (*psychological message*)

Tom: 'Did they? Well, OK I'll book you on it straight away'

Figure 4.6 An angular transaction

Note the use in Figure 4.6 of a broken line to signify the psychological ulterior covert nature of communication at this level. In the case of angular transactions, the 'angling' of the communication is always deliberate and in Adult awareness, and is used extensively by anyone wishing to persuade or convince another, particularly by such professionals as salesmen, management consultants, teachers and therapists. Consider the following example:

Management consultant: 'Yes, Company X have been using our approach with some success [A–A social message] 'You're not keeping up with the others!' [A–C psychological message]

Client: 'Hmm, really. Tell me more about it. Your approach may well be something we can use' [C–A response]

DUPLEX TRANSACTIONS

These are also complex transactions with an ulterior message alongside a social one, this time involving four rather than three ego states. The example from our story is the final exchange, shown in Figure 4.7. The first ulterior message, from Tom to Ted, is, 'I'm going to give you a rollicking'; and the second from Ted to Tom, 'Yes, I'll let you clobber me'.

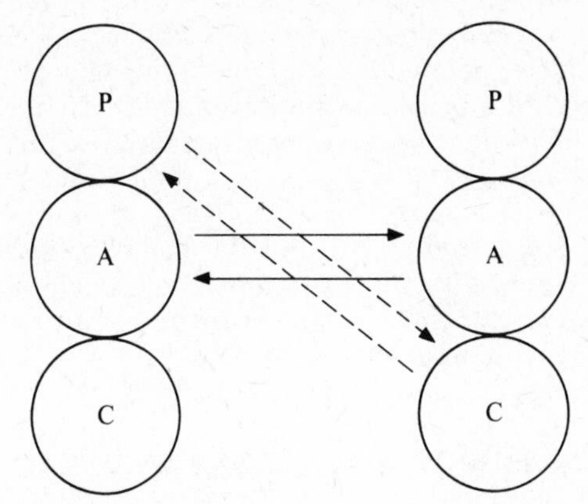

Tom: 'Come into my office for a chat' (*social message*) 'I'm going to give you a rollicking' (*psychological message*)

Ted: 'Yes, OK then' (*social message*) 'Yes, I'll let you clobber me' (*psychological message*)

Figure 4.7 A duplex transaction

Not all duplex transactions lead to trouble, but this one was almost bound to. Many rewarding relationships have duplex transactions and they add to the richness of human contact. However, some signal the start of a transactional sequence called a game (see Chapter 7) which usually has unpleasant outcomes for one or both parties. Unlike angular transactions, duplex transactions often occur without Adult awareness.

RULES OF COMMUNICATION

Using the idea of transactions it is possible to draw up some 'rules of communication' as guidelines to interaction between people.

1 As long as the transactions are complementary, communication may continue indefinitely
2 If there is a change to a crossed transaction, a break in the flow of communication may occur, perhaps only very briefly, with the likelihood of something different happening afterwards
3 The outcome of ulterior transactions is determined at the psychological level and not at the social.

For example, the extent to which crossed transactions break up communication between people depends a lot on the nature of their relationship and the subject matter of their exchange. It is possible for two close friends to 'spar' with one another using many crossed transactions. However, if a breakdown in communication does occur it is always worth looking for the crossed transaction. Also, the recipient of an ulterior transaction, whether angular or duplex, can choose not to give the 'expected' response. Psychological messages abound in human relationships, adding to both the complexity and richness, which is why it can be difficult to diagnose an ego state from only one word or gesture as a clue. In any case, we are frequently operating from more than one ego state at any given time.

IMPLICATIONS FOR ORGANISATIONS AND TRAINING

Difficulties in relationships and inadequate communication between people are seen as a major cause of poor performance by organisations. At least, this belief is widely shared by both managers and trainers alike, with some anecdotal support, but less in the way of systematic factual evidence. In addition, many organisations see it as an explicit or implicit value that communication skills are a subject worthy of attention in management development and training, together with all the quantitative disciplines. The analysis of transactions offers us a model for looking at the communication issue that is both simple enough to teach relatively quickly and flexible enough to account for a wide range of possible responses. It provides guidelines for the improvement of relations (spotting the crossed transaction), and avoiding being put down and losing personal and job effectiveness (deliberately crossing the transaction).

REFERENCE

1 P. McCormick, *Social Transactions,* Transactional Publications, 1977.

5 Life positions

Another way of looking at relationships between people is through the concept of 'life position', sometimes referred to as the basic position or existential position. A person's life position at any given time expresses in some way just how that individual is relating to others in terms of thinking, feeling and behaving. There are four basic life positions, shown in Figure 5.1 referred to as the OK corral.[1]

Figure 5.1 OK corral

I'm not OK You're OK	I'm OK You're OK
I'm not OK You're not OK	I'm OK You're not OK

EXAMPLES OF LIFE POSITIONS

The idea of life positions can be demonstrated using the following examples.

1. 'Hey, we did a good job there', says the boss
   'Yes, things are really going well for us now', says the subordinate
   [I'm OK, you're OK]
2. 'Your work is not up to the standard I need in this department!' says the boss
   [I'm OK, you're not OK]
3. 'I wish I could keep on top of things the way you can', says the subordinate
   [I'm not OK, you're OK]
4. 'Well, I don't know what to do and you don't know what to do. What a mess!' says the boss
   [I'm not OK, you're not OK]

CHARACTERISTICS OF THE LIFE POSITIONS

I'M OK, YOU'RE OK (I+ U+)

This is sometimes referred to as the *get on with* position. People occupying this position are optimistic, confident and happy about work and life. They use time constructively, doing the things they most want to. They exchange strokes freely with those they meet, accepting the significance of other people, and decline to put themselves or others down. They are assertive in reaching their aims, i.e. they state and elaborate their own views and needs rather than attack other people's views and needs. Their dominant working style with others is collaboration and mutual respect, sharing authority and responsibility and listening constructively, even if they disagree. The problems they encounter in work and life are faced and dealt with as constructively as possible. They are likely to 'succeed' in life within the limits they've set themselves, finding satisfaction with work and relationships, and tend to live long, healthy lives.

I'M OK, YOU'RE NOT OK (I+ U−)

This is sometimes referred to as the *get rid of* position. It is characterised by feelings of anger, fury and hostility. Others are seen as inferior, unworthy, incompetent, wrong and not to be trusted. Behaviour to others is characterised by such things as spite, victimisation, trapping, condescension, abuse and disregard. They may devote much time to the destruction of the sense of self-worth of others. As well as putting others down, they over-inflate their own self-worth, deny personal problems and find it difficult to give positive strokes. At work they are highly competitive and climb over others at whatever cost to achieve power and status. In wider social terms this is the life position of those who exploit their fellow man, or of those who take dogmatic views, believing theirs to be the only right course. In extreme cases they are homicidal ('You are so "not OK", there's no point to your living').

I'M NOT OK, YOU'RE OK (I− U+)

This is referred to as the *get away from* position and is typified by feelings such as sadness, inadequacy, stupidity or a sense of being ugly. In this position, people experience themselves as inferior or powerless in relation to others. They put themselves down and find it difficult to accept positive strokes, even being suspicious of them. In relation to work, they undervalue their potential and skills and they avoid or withdraw from difficult situations and problems. In life generally, they don't succeed, are unhappy, often ill and/or depressed and in extreme cases commit suicide ('I'm so useless I may as well not live').

I'M NOT OK, YOU'RE NOT OK (I− U−)

This is also referred to as the *get nowhere position* and is accompanied by feelings of confusion or aimlessness and pointlessness. Their attitude is 'Why bother, what's the point?' and they frequently waste time. They do nothing very much in life, and in extreme cases become alcoholics or drug addicts, or go crazy, possibly committing murder or suicide.

THE ORIGINS OF LIFE POSITIONS

According to Berne, the newborn baby is fundamentally in an 'I'm OK, you're OK' position (unless perhaps there is some genetic defect present) and only switches from this under pressure of early experiences. This view is based on trust being the starting position of the infant, and that at birth 'all things are possible' until this trust is interfered with. Harris[2] on the other hand views the birth position as 'I'm not OK, you're OK', perhaps highlighted by the new baby's dependence on those around (particularly mother) for food, warmth, strokes, etc. Either way, the general view in TA is that a person's basic life position is established at about three to four years old.

Of particular importance are the circumstances that result in the formation of an 'I'm OK, you're not OK' life position.[3] In its more severe form, this is the life position of the exploiter, crusader, criminal and psychopath. Such personalities can wreak havoc and destruction in societies if they achieve power (e.g. Hitler). If that power is the leadership of our organisations the consequences can still be severe (disregard for others and the mores of society, embezzlement and crooked deals, and exploitation of those around them). So, a greater understanding of the formation of the 'I'm OK, you're not OK' life position could be of significant help in terms of developing more collaborative, more compassionate and less destructive societies.

People vary considerably in terms of their 'mobility' through the life positions and also the severity of their experience in each of the 'not-OK' ones. One individual may move rapidly through all four within the space of twenty-four hours with 'mild' experiences (some joy, some sadness, some anger, some sense of futility). He or she is not prevented from functioning in society and at work, although at times their job effectiveness may suffer.

On the other hand, another individual may spend most of his life in 'severe' circumstances in one life position, e.g. a hospitalised schizophrenic in the 'I'm not OK, you're not OK' position. While 'I'm OK, you're OK' as a fundamental life view is worthy of attainment (and most of us experience more 'not-OK-ness' than is helpful to healthy relationships), it does seem something of an ideal on a twenty-four hours per day, seven days per week basis. However, it is certainly a valid, if implicit, aim of good approaches to education, training, therapy and rehabilitation. TA certainly takes the view that people can move to a dominantly 'I'm OK, you're OK' position, even late in life.

There are thus four dimensions of relevance to life positions:

I – you
OK – not OK
mobility ('How rapidly do I change life position')
severity ('How extreme is my behaviour in my life position').

IMPLICATIONS FOR ORGANISATIONS AND TRAINING

It sometimes seems that our organisations foster and experience more competition within them than between them. Certainly many organisations are rife with covert, manipulative and 'political' behaviour in which those with an 'I'm OK, you're not OK' life position very often scramble to the top of the pile at the expense of others, irrespective of competence. And yet it may not be the most desirable state of affairs in terms of human dignity, individual growth and organisational effectiveness, since power and exploitation are likely to take precedence over work and collaboration. Many senior managers who see their workers as inherently 'not OK' do indeed get 'not-OK' behaviour as a response ('Well, if that's the way they see us, that's the way we'll be'). They may even be recruiting to fulfil these perceptions (unconsciously, of course).

Moving an organisation to a largely 'I'm OK, you're OK' position demands a major organisational development intervention, with a high focus on interpersonal relationships and team building. As far as interpersonal skills trainers are concerned, operating from either a 'You're not OK' position or 'I'm not OK' position in relation to trainees is likely to lead to reduced effectiveness in their work.

Participants on interpersonal skill training courses do not usually exhibit extreme forms of 'not-OK-ness'. If they do, the trainer needs to be very clear about his interventions with such people and he always has the choice of advising someone to see a therapist. The 'You're not OK' life position of trainees seems to present the most difficulties for trainers since people with this as a dominant position:

1. Frequently nominate others for training, but not themselves ('After all, I'm OK, I've made it, it's those useless so-and-so's down there that need it!')
2. If they do go on a course, frequently attack the trainer and are resistant to feedback ('Why should I listen to you, you're only a trainer').

REFERENCES

1 F.H. Ernst, 'The OK corral: The grid for get-on-with', *Transactional Analysis Journal,* vol. 1, no. 4, 1971.
2 T.A. Harris, *I'm OK, You're OK,* Harper and Row, 1969; Pan Books Ltd., 1973.
3 F. English, 'What shall I do tomorrow' in *Transactional Analysis After Eric Berne,* G. Barnes, (ed), Harper's College Press, 1977.

6 Time structuring

In the early years of the meetings of the San Francisco Seminar, a question that occupied the attention of the participants was: 'How do we spend our time in relation to others?' These deliberations led to the view that there are six ways of structuring our time between birth and death (Figure 6.1). The choice we make at a given time will depend on the situation we face and also our early experiences in childhood (see Chapter 9). For example, some people find it difficult to get close to others (intimacy) and spend most of their time engaged in rituals and pastimes.

Figure 6.1 Time structuring

Withdrawal	No contact with others
Rituals	Socially programmed exchanges, e.g. 'Good morning, how are you?'
Pastimes	Superficial exchanges about non-threatening subjects, e.g. sport
Activity	External goal-directed behaviour, e.g. work, hobbies
Games	Recurring transactions with a concealed motivation
Intimacy	Game free honesty and openness, free of exploitation

WITHDRAWAL

This is the choice of having no contact with others (sometimes sleeping and meditation are included under withdrawal). It may be purposeful and deliberate, based on an Adult ego state decision. For example, manager X may decide to relax at home, by reading, watching television, or taking a hot bath. Manager Y may decide to withdraw at work, by shutting himself in his office to think and plan before starting a project or going to a meeting.

Most people appear to need some time on their own although the extent varies considerably. A minority of people are very gregarious, seeking constant companionship, while others seem to want little contact, seeking tasks such as sailing singlehanded round the world and jobs like night watchman and lighthouse keeper.

In some situations, withdrawal may be dysfunctional, for example avoiding a difficult person, problem or situation that has to be faced. Some people withdraw as an Adapted Child response rather than confront their difficulties, perhaps in the hope that they will go away, and others habitually withdraw in the face of conflict or anger. A clear example in an organisation is someone leaving a meeting when the atmosphere becomes uncomfortable and tense. A very common response is mental withdrawal rather than physical, for example 'switching off' during a boring lecture.

RITUALS

Rituals are highly predictable and formalised exchanges between people based on social custom and they are important in holding the fabric of society together. They may be complex, as for example a coronation or an election, or simple, as in the following greetings:

Manager X: 'Good morning, how are you?'
Manager Y: 'I'm fine, nice to see you!'

The basis of a ritual is that everyone is agreeing to do the same thing during that time. As in the greeting above, rituals may be sincere, but usually do not involve much commitment or closeness, and are frequently instantaneous, based on social habit. They can be specific to groups and organisations. However sophisticated an organisation's approach to induction training, a task for any new recruit is to discover the extant rituals with the minimum of embarrassment. Discomfort and even anger may occur when a time-honoured ritual is broken in some way, as in the example:

Manager X: 'Good morning!'
Manager Y: 'What's good about it!'

PASTIMES

Pastimes are a way of structuring time around topics of mutual interest. They offer little threat and operate as a means to get to know people and decide whether or not to form closer friendships and/or to do business together. They are also important for self confirmation, i.e. re-affirming who we are, what interest groups we belong to and our status in society. They typically occur at parties and other social gatherings, and also at teabreaks and mealtimes at work. Some examples[1] include: General Motors, who won? (both 'man talk'); grocery, wardrobe, nappies ('woman talk'); how to (go about something); how much? (does it cost); ever been? (to somewhere); do you know? (so and so); and morning after (what a hangover!).

Ability in pastiming is viewed as a highly important attribute in society and a basic part of being 'socially competent'. In some selling situations, pastiming is an important skill necessary for the effective execution of the job itself.

Not having pastiming skills may be a serious disadvantage in developing relationships with others. Because of their lack of pastiming skills, some people are seen as being either withdrawn or 'coming on' too strong and scaring other people off. On the other hand, some people never get beyond pastiming with others and thus never form close relationships.

ACTIVITIES

Activity is any behaviour directed towards external goals, such as hobbies and sport, household activities (e.g. sewing, building a drive), social activities (organising the tennis club's annual dance) and work. The latter is, of course, the most prized way of time structuring as far as the organisation (or at least the managing director) is concerned, but the other forms of time structuring are likely to be occurring at the same time.

Activities can be very satisfying in themselves through creativity or productivity and very rewarding because of the strokes gained from others. Some people use activity to avoid contact with others, working all hours possible and making decisions and money instead of friends. In modern technological society much activity at work is loaded with negative strokes because of its dehumanised, undignified and repetitive qualities.

GAMES

Unlike the preceding forms of time structuring, which may involve any ego state, the Adult and Free Child are excluded from games. Games are almost always considered negative in some way and are discussed in Chapter 7.

INTIMACY

Intimacy is a state characterised by:

spontaneity
honesty, trust, candidness
shared feelings, thoughts and experiences
heightened awareness
no ulterior transactions, no games
access to all three ego states.

It is essentially a function of the Free Child, and seems to be innately present in infants until or unless parental influences interfere. It is unpredictable and unprogrammed and can be risky and frightening, with the potential for personal rejection (when we open ourselves up to someone else, we may not get an open response back). It can occur in the midst of a crowd, in a continuing friendship, in a marriage and at work. It seems impossible to maintain continuously.[2]

Intimacy occurs not only in the context of sexual, emotional , aesthetic, recreational and spiritual activity,[2] but also in such areas pertinent to organisations as:

work and the sharing of common tasks
commitment and joint investment in common goals
conflict, where there is a mutual concern and effort to resolve difficulties and problems
creativity and thought, where there is joint involvement in the development of new ideas.

TIME STRUCTURING AND STROKES

Generally the stroke intensity received from others increases from withdrawal (no strokes from others) through to intimacy, the richest source of strokes. In withdrawal, there may be intense internal stroking of the Child ego state by the influencing Parent. The strokes from rituals and pastimes are sometimes referred to as maintenance strokes – when we are feeling stroke-deprived, they can give us some support in maintaining our sense of 'OK-ness'. Games are largely a source of negative strokes. People who are scared of intimacy may have to indulge in a lot of rituals and pastimes, or spend all their time in work (activity) to make up for it.

IMPLICATIONS FOR ORGANISATIONS AND TRAINING

The idea of time structuring has some interesting implications for organisations. The ways managers spend their time has long been a topic of interest[3] and the use of diaries has been an intervention in management development for some years now. By diagnosing his/her use of time, a manager may be able to separate its constructive from its non-constructive use, and hence make better decisions. Time structuring may well add another very useful dimension to that diagnosis. Certainly some senior managers imagine or wish that their staff would spend all their time at work involved solely in activity. Since many jobs have a high component of working with and through people, this is an impossible demand for a healthy work life and a healthy and productive organisation. It's interesting that time sheets (for recording the hours spent in different work aspects or projects) used by some organisations for accounting purposes assume employees are engaged in activity all the time!

From a trainer's viewpoint it may be possible to relate different management styles to different ways of structuring time as shown in Figure 6.2, in a way that relates to other theories of management style.[4] As far as running courses is concerned, time structuring emphasises the need for participants to get to know each other, through the rituals and pastimes of course introductions, before starting the main work.

Figure 6.2 Time structuring and management style

Preferred mode of time structuring	*Style of management*
Withdrawal	Avoiding contact and abdicating responsibility
Rituals	Over-reliance on set ways of doing things
Pastimes	Over-reliance on smooth, superficial relationships
Activity	Putting the job and production before people
Above as appropriate plus intimacy	Balancing relationships and tasks for maximum effectiveness and satisfaction

REFERENCES

1 E. Berne, *Games People Play,* Grove Press Inc., 1964; Penguin, 1968.
2 J.P. Anderson, *A Transactional Analysis Primer,* Annual Handbook for Group Facilitators, University Associates, 1973.
3 R. Stewart, *Managers and their Jobs,* Macmillan, 1967.
4 R.R. Blake and J.S. Mouton, *Building a Dynamic Corporation through Grid Organisation Development,* Addison-Wesley, 1969.

7 Games

DEFINITION

Games[1] are a form of time structuring, based on a particular kind of transaction involving two or more people. They were defined by Berne as 'an ongoing series of complementary ulterior transactions progressing to a well-defined predictable outcome'. They are special for two reasons: first, they are perhaps the most publicised aspect of TA due to the popularity of *Games People Play;* and second, they have several distinct characteristics.

1. They have a repetitive quality, i.e. the same people keep playing the same games, sometimes with a great sense of deja vu ('Oh, it's happened to me again!')
2. They are predictable, i.e. when the first move (verbal or non-verbal) is made in a game, the 'die is cast' the outcome assured, unless the parties are enlightened and aware and spot what's happening
3. They are ulterior, i.e. to say there is an explicit social message, and also a covert psychological message. (However not all ulterior transactions lead to games by any means)
4. They are learnt behaviours, acquired during childhood
5. Game players intuitively seek out corresponding partners, suggesting that they are initiated by the Little Professor, without Adult awareness
6. In a game, somebody is put down and both parties end up with a 'bad feeling'. A 'bad feeling' has a particular meaning in TA, namely a feeling gained by putting someone down or being put down. For example, the feeling may be sadness, inadequacy, confusion or fright (when put down) or anger, smugness or superiority (when putting someone else down).

The notion of games encapsulates a situation all too common in human experience, sometimes vivid, involving intense feelings and dramatic consequences. This chapter conveys the essence of games through examples and concepts.

THE NATURE OF GAMES

Figure 7.1 illustrates the game of 'Now I've got you, you son of a bitch' (referred to as NIGYSOB). The boss appears to be acting from his Adult, but in fact is setting up a situation so he can give his secretary a hefty negative stroke using his Critical Parent. This highlights a fundamental aspect of games. People get into the habit of playing them without being fully aware of what they are doing and personal awareness is a key requirement for breaking them. If Sally comes away from this encounter with a sense of deja vu and a sense of receiving the same old bad feelings (inadequacy or sadness for example) the likelihood is that she regularly gets involved in this game. Games are at least a source of 'trouble', because they get in the way of getting close to people (intimacy) and doing effective work (activity) and can be highly destructive, even fatal, as in drug addiction and alcoholism. Each of us usually has one or two favourite games, the type of game depending on our preferred life position. Those who have an 'I'm not OK' life position are likely to play 'victim' games. Some typical 'victim' games are:

Kick me ('I'm so bad, kick me!')
Poor me ('The whole world is against me')
Stupid ('I'm so stupid I can't understand *anything*')
Wooden leg ('I could do so much if it weren't for my . . .')
Harried ('I always have to work so hard and be in such a rush').

Figure 7.1 The game of NIGYSOB

Boss:	'Have you got the Smith report, Sally?'
Secretary:	'Yes'
Boss:	'That's good, it's very important and I knew I could trust you to keep an eye on it'
Secretary:	Looks in filing cabinet and becomes increasingly embarrassed because she cannot find the report. Finally, she says, 'I'm dreadfully sorry but I just don't seem to be able to find it'
Boss:	'I'm not surprised, it has been sent to me by Mr Williams' (Reveals report with a flourish) 'who found it amongst some papers you sent to him by mistake. We'll need to talk about this at your annual appraisal!'

A 'victim' sets up a situation to receive negative strokes. This is clearly shown in Figure 7.2 where a new secretary is playing the game of 'Stupid'.

Figure 7.2 The game of Stupid

New secretary:	'Can you tell me how this filing system works again please?'
Experienced secretary:	'What you need to do is . . .'
New secretary:	'Oh, er, I'm still a bit uncertain. Do you mean that . . .?'
Experienced secretary:	'No! It's a question of . . .'
New secretary:	'Oh dear, I'm rather silly, aren't I?'
Experienced secretary:	'Well, it was designed to be a simple system and nobody's had problems understanding it before!'

Victim players seek out people who play 'persecutor' or 'rescuer' games. 'Persecutors' have a life position of I+ U−. Typical persecutor games are:

NIGYSOB ('I'm really going to put you down') (see Figure 7.1)
Blemish ('I can *always* find a mistake in whatever you have done')
Let's you and him fight ('I think you ought to go and have a fight with him . . . can I watch?')
Schlemiel ('I'm going to test your powers of tolerance by making lots and lots and lots of mistakes').

Rescuer players also operate from a life position of I+ U−. Some typical rescuer games are:

I'm only trying to help you ('How could you be so ungrateful after all I've done for you?')
What would you do without me ('You're incapable of looking after yourself')
They'll be glad they knew me ('I'm having a miserable time looking after everybody but myself. Still, I'm sure they'll appreciate it in the end').

The rescuer works on the basic assumption that his or her main purpose in life is to look after others and that the world is full of people who are inadequate and need to be helped in spite of themselves. As with persecutors, rescuers seek out victims. This is shown in Figure 7.3 where the 'adviser' is playing a game of 'After all I've done for you'.

Figure 7.3 'After all I've done for you'

Adviser:	'Wonderful news Mr Smith, I've finally been able to solve your problem! I know you said that you were rather uncertain about taking a job abroad but I've been able to line up a marvellous two-year job for you in Saudi Arabia'
Mr Smith:	'Well . . . er . . . I'm . . .'
Adviser:	'Come now Mr Smith, it really is an excellent opportunity and you'll be able to come back to Britain for two months each year'
Mr Smith:	'Well I'm not happy about it'
Adviser:	'Well really! After all the effort I've put into this, I do think you are being very ungrateful!'

Our society claims to value help, caring and support for others. The problem is that rescuing tends to keep others in a very dependent relationship, with little opportunity for self-development and responsibility, whereas true helping aims to give us at least some degree of independence and self-responsibility. Rescuing and true helping can be very easily confused making it sometimes difficult to spot and confront rescuing games.

THE DRAMA TRIANGLE[2]

The roles of persecutor (P), rescuer (R) and victim (V) together form the drama triangle (Figure 7.4). The basic idea here is that we tend to have a favourite role (persecutor, rescuer or victim), but we may switch very rapidly in a situation involving games. This is illustrated in the following domestic scene.

A man hears the married couple next door having a row. He decides to knock on their door to see if he can help (*rescuer*). The door is flung open and he sees the wife crying (*victim*) and the husband red with rage (*persecutor*). The neighbour starts to explain that he wondered if he could help, when the wife starts screaming (*persecutor*) at him and tells him to mind his own business. The husband joins in (he clings to his

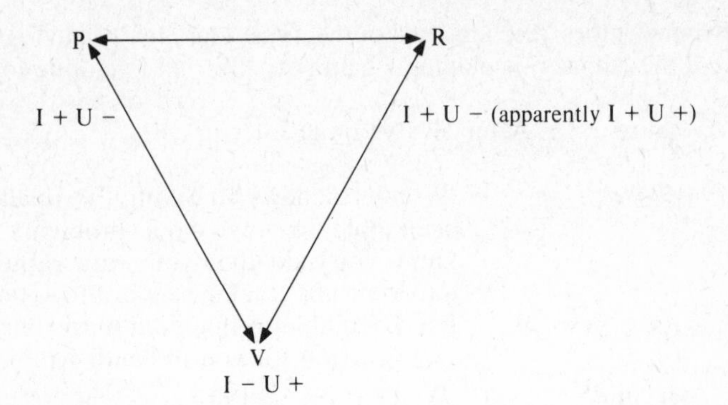

Figure 7.4 The drama triangle

persecutor role) and the neighbour, mumbling apologies, retreats to the safety of his home (*victim*).

THE CONSEQUENCES AND PAYOFFS OF GAMES

By playing games, people:

- avoid responsibility for the problems they have
- avoid the risks in being close to and open with others
- make people and situations more predictable
- exchange negative strokes (see Chapter 3)
- structure time in a predictable way (see Chapter 6)
- keep re-experiencing a favourite bad feeling (known as a racket – see Chapter 8)
- confirm a life position (see Chapter 5)
- further their life plan (known as a script – see Chapter 9).

INTENSITY OF GAMES

A game can be an isolated incident, or it can happen with such frequency that it reflects a whole orientation to life. For example, one serious victim game is 'Alcoholic'.[3] Here the player spends his life in a continuous round of going on binges, feeling repentant, drying out and then drinking too much again. 'Alcoholic' is a third degree game. In third degree games, individuals end up by damaging themselves and/or others (e.g. cirrhosis of the liver from alcoholism). Second degree games are less destructive, but they are sufficiently intense to cause a good deal of bad feelings. A second degree 'harried' player will always be in a rush working hard and never give himself time to get close to people. In this case, he can always, always play for higher stakes, become a third degree 'harried' player and have a heart attack at forty-five. First degree games are mild and usually only lead to mild discomfort. For example, a boss who is a first degree 'blemish' player, and frequently criticises his staff for using full stops when they should use semi-colons, will probably be regarded at best with amusement and at worst as pedantic.

STOPPING GAMES

Awareness is the key to handling and stopping games. For all games there is a psychological ulterior message which is different from the social message. The social message may be Adult initiated, but it is actually the psychological message 'underneath' that determines the outcome (third rule of communication – see Chapter 4). This is illustrated in Figure 7.5 which gives the likely opening moves in the complementary games of NIGYSOB (boss) and 'Kick me' (subordinate). In handling or stopping a game an immediate and often productive option is to comment on the apparent psychological message. In this example it would mean the subordinate, using his Adult, saying something like, 'You sound as if you really want to tell me off'. The subordinate would thus be inviting the boss to be direct and 'straight' with him. Equally the boss could avoid initiating the game. To do this he would need to make sure he did not send a double message. Using his Adult or his Parent he could simply say, 'I am angry with you because . . .'.

One way to increase our awareness and avoid games if we find that we frequently come away from particular situations with 'bad' feelings, is to use a transactional diagram to see what has happened and prepare to take a different approach the next time. As well as increasing our awareness, and hence choices, we can reduce our involvement in games by:

- declining to put ourselves and others down
- declining to exaggerate our own and others' weaknesses and strengths
- refusing to move into a persecutor, rescuing or victim position
- exchanging genuine positive strokes
- spending more time in activity and intimacy (although harried players need to spend less time in activity).

S_1 'Will you pop into my office?'
R_1 'Yes, I'll come straight away' } *social message*

S_2 'I'm going to clobber you'
R_2 'I'll come and be kicked' } *covert/psychological message*

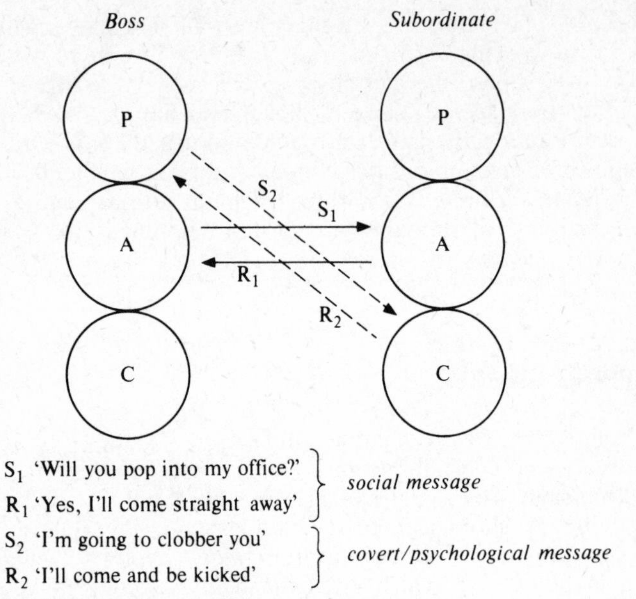

Figure 7.5 Transactional diagram of a game

THE GAME FORMULA

The transactional diagram (Figure 7.5) shows a game situation from an ego-state viewpoint and the drama triangle (Figure 7.4), from a life-position viewpoint. Another way to consider the mechanics of games is the game formula (Figure 7.6), originally developed by Berne.[4]

Figure 7.6 Game formula

$$C + G = R \rightarrow S \rightarrow X \rightarrow P$$

con+gimmick → = response → switch → crossup → pay-off

(switch → crossup → pay-off: may be simultaneous)

This formula illustrates a game between person A and person B as follows. The game is initiated by A's discount (i.e. put down of self or other), referred to as the *con.* A's Little Professor has already spotted intuitively that B is a likely partner for the game about to unfold. If B does respond accordingly to the secret message by also discounting, he or she reveals the part of him/her that is interested in being 'hooked' by the con, and referred to as the *gimmick.* A series of social transactions then follow, usually Adult to Adult, referred to as the *response.* At some point, each player *switches,* i.e. they drop the facade of the social messages and demonstrate explicitly the previously hidden messages, together with the ego states involved. At this point, a moment of confusion (the *crossup*), perhaps very brief, may be experienced by each person, followed by the *pay-off,* i.e. the 'bad feelings'. As an example, consider the moves in the first game to be extensively analysed by Berne shown in Figure 7.7.

Figure 7.7 The game of 'Why don't you . . . yes but'

Boss (social message)	: 'Well, we've got a catastrophe on our hands, any ideas?'	
[Con	: Why don't you see if you can come up with a solution I can't find fault with?]	
Subordinate (social message)	: 'Why don't you . . .'	
[Gimmick	: There's no problem I can't solve, I'll sort your problems out]	
Boss	: 'Yes, but they'd never agree . . .'	[Responses]
Subordinate	: 'What if . . .'	
Boss	: 'Oh, that would cost too much'	
Subordinate	: 'How about . . .	
Boss	: 'C'mon, we tried that three years ago, and it got us nowhere'	
Boss	: 'You know, I was expecting something better from you!'	
[Switch, followed by crossup	: Boss, in Critical Parent, demonstrating inadequacy of subordinate. Subordinate in Adapted Child ego state, looking crestfallen]	
[Payoff	: Boss feels superior: 'He really is useless' Subordinate feels inadequate, despondent; 'I just don't seem to be able to produce the goods!']	

IMPLICATIONS FOR ORGANISATIONS AND TRAINERS

Because of their destructive quality, games in organisations waste energy, time and money. The competitive, as opposed to collaborative, ethos rampant in many of our organisations often supports the extensive playing of games during 'firm's time'. Most employees probably do not spend much of their time in games, but the time that is so spent

Figure 7.8 Some games played in organisations

Title of game	*Mythical belief underlying the game (thesis)*	*What the player gets by starting the game (pay-off)*
Ain't it awful	Misery loves company	Collects sympathy
Blemish	There is always something wrong with everyone and everything else	Avoids exposure of own problems by finding 'blemishes'
Corner	You're damned if you do and damned if you don't	Triumph in getting the other person in the corner, feeling bad
Harried	I've got to do everything right, and what's more, I've got to do it right away	Incapacitation, e.g. collapse with exhaustion, nervous breakdown, coronary, ulcers
If it weren't for you	There's always someone who stops me doing what I want to	Avoiding doing what he/she 'wants to do', but actually fears
I'm only trying to help you	Nobody ever takes my advice	Bewilderment and confusion at ungrateful people
Intellectual Rapo	Gee, you're wonderful professor	Setting the 'professor' (expert) up and then chopping them down later, so that they feel inadequate
Kick me	How come this always happens to me?	Rejection, hurt, inadequacy, sadness
Let's you and him fight	I always seem to get left out	Setting up an argument or fight, and then withdrawing from it
Look how hard I've tried	You can't tell me what to do	Proving that he or she can't be helped or blamed
Mine's better than yours	Well I'm OK, because, after all, I am better than you/they	Avoids feeling inadequate
Now I've got you, you son of a bitch	I can make everyone and anyone feel bad	Triumph in putting others down and avoidance of thinking about own problems
Rapo	Men/women are only after one thing	Proving the opposite sex is no good

Schlemiel	I can do some pretty terrible things and still be forgiven	Getting forgiveness
See what you made me do	It's never my fault, always yours	Making others feel guilty about the mistakes he/she makes
Stupid	As long as I'm stupid, everyone will feel satisfied	Proving he/she can't think and hence avoiding responsibility
Uproar	If we make enough noise and put enough space between us, we won't have to solve the problem	Angry withdrawal, hence avoiding intimacy
Why don't you . . . yes, but	Whatever solution you come up with, I bet I can find a fault	Proving others are inadequate or inferior
Wooden leg	Well, what do you expect from someone with a wooden leg like mine! (i.e. some real or imagined physical or social disability)	Demonstrating that he/she has no responsibility for own problems

may be critical in terms of the reduced quality and effectiveness of relationships and work. Some games are particularly destructive. For example, harried players are often supported in their game by organisations ('He works so hard, let's promote him') taking on more and more responsibilities and work, without taking care of themselves. They eventually collect a final pay-off, leaving at least temporarily a 'hole' in the organisation. For example, the harried playing senior executive has his nervous breakdown or coronary leaving everyone to scrabble around trying to pick up the pieces of the thousand-and-one jobs he had in hand. Alcoholic is also very serious, as the alcoholic manager is rarely effective, and historically has posed considerable problems for organisations in terms of who is responsible for what is done about him and how he is to be treated. As far as trainers are concerned, those involved in interpersonal skills training can help participants to focus on destructive and self-limiting aspects of their behaviour through the concept of games, and help them choose more effective ways of relating to others. In some instances, this may mean advising, counselling or therapy. Trainers, of whatever specialism, sometimes get into games with participants in training sessions. An awareness of games, together with some choices for dealing with them, may help to minimise this particular block to training effectiveness.

REFERENCES

1 E. Berne, *Games People Play*, Grove Press Inc., 1964; Penguin, 1968.
2 S. Karpman, 'Fairy tales and script drama analysis', *Transactional Analysis Bulletin*, vol. 7, no. 26, 1968.
3 C. Steiner, *Games Alcoholics Play*, Grove Press Inc., 1971.
4 E. Berne, *What Do You Say After You Say Hello?* Grove Press Inc., 1972; Corgi, 1975.

8 Rackets and stamps

RACKETS

The chairman called his executive directors together for an important board meeting, prior to the publication of the half-yearly reports. 'Well gentlemen', he said smiling, 'we've had a good six months and my congratulations to you all for your support and effort.' All but one of his fellow directors relaxed and smiled with him. 'However, good though the results are, they're not good enough', he said slowly and grimly. 'I must call on you and your staff to put more effort in during the next six months!'

> the managing director felt confused
> the sales and marketing director felt inadequate
> the production director felt guilty
> the research and development director felt miserable
> the administration director felt scared
> the financial director felt angry and started to think which one of his colleagues to blame
> the wise old personnel director noticed each of his colleagues getting into their racket feelings . . . and kept his own counsel.

In this little story, all but one of the directors were 'caught' by the chairman and ended up in their 'racket' or 'racket feeling', i.e. the bad feeling pay-off at the end of a game. Many people are likely to have one particular racket and consequently it is sometimes referred to as their 'favourite bad feeling'. For example, some individuals have anger, while others have depression, confusion, hurt, fear, or inadequacy. Any feeling may be a racket feeling. Some people seem to have more than one racket feeling, whereas a few don't seem to have one at all.

DIFFERENCE BETWEEN RACKET AND 'REAL' OR REACTIVE FEELINGS

Racket feelings are Adapted Child substitutes for spontaneous Free Child feelings which in some way are not permitted in our early years. Both are instantaneous and both are really felt. However, there are some important differences, as shown in Figure 8.1.

Figure 8.1 Racket and real feelings

Racket feelings	*Real (reactive) feelings*
Arise from Adapted Child	Arise from Free Child
Learnt, substitute way of getting strokes	Spontaneous
Often experienced by others as manipulative and false	Usually experienced by others as authentic
Repetitive, with no useful action taken by individual	Once expressed, are done with, and individual moves on to fresh business

Rackets are considered as being learnt under the influence of one or more of the following processes:[1]

1 Straight modelling for a child by a parent, i.e. a racket is passed on by example
2 By stroking into a child's behaviour, e.g. only paying attention to a child when he/she is sad, for example
3 By telling a child what to feel or think (e.g. an angry child is told, 'You're tired and need to go to bed' – a notorious example – with the development of a 'tiredness' racket).

STAMPS

Stamps (or to give them their full title, trading stamps) are feelings that an individual collects and stores rather than expressing at the instant they were experienced. These feelings are discharged at a later date. Consider the following example. Bill Smith was production manager at the Symbiosis Drug Company. His job was challenging, stimulating and tough. On Monday, one of his foremen was late for the fourth time in a month and volunteered a trivial excuse. Bill said nothing. On Tuesday, the quality control department checked the same batch twice by mistake. Bill said nothing. On Wednesday someone damaged a fork lift truck and on Thursday one of the suppliers sent the wrong material. On Friday his secretary missed a sentence from a memo to the managing director and Bill finally lost his temper. His unfortunate secretary bore the brunt of it.

Bill Smith had been saving anger stamps all week, and on the last day he cashed them in with a great outburst. Psychological trading stamps are so called because of certain parallels to the commercial variety.

1 They are collected and stored until some future date (Mon-

day to Friday for Bill Smith)

2 Different individuals collect different types. Some people collect bad feelings (brown stamps) and some people good feelings (gold stamps). The bad feelings collected may be even more specific, e.g. anger (red stamps, as for Bill Smith) or depression (blue stamps), guilt, hurt, etc.

3 Eventually the stamps are redeemed. Different people collect different quantities and have different compulsions as to when, where and how they redeem them. Some cash them in for a small prize, e.g. throwing a rubber at the wall, losing temper with someone else over a small mistake, taking a day off. Others cash them in for a big prize such as taking company property (brown stamps), firing an employee (brown stamps) or taking a week's holiday (gold stamps). Sometimes the prize can be really big, for example losing the company a lot of money, getting fired, having a breakdown or even a suicide. In all cases this cashing in or redemption time is accompanied by a sense of justification, which is often indicated by the phrases a person uses, e.g. 'I couldn't stand it any more'; 'That's the last straw'; 'Given all that's happened, what else was there to do?'

4 Some people review their stamps extensively (for instance, go over all their hurts and angers before going to sleep at night), while others 'put them away in drawer' and forget about them for weeks, months or even years. Sometimes people review their collections with one another and by this means pick up 'secondary stamps' on behalf of others, e.g. 'Is that what he said to you?; of all the nerve, that makes me really angry!'

In origin stamp collecting is a learnt behaviour, sited in the Adapted Child. Some people pick up their stamps from imaginary transactions in the first place, as opposed to real transactions. Not only is stamp collecting a bar to autonomous behaviour and expression by the collector, it can also be a serious hindrance to effective working relationships. For example, the boss who collects anger stamps and cashes them in for a free rave at his subordinates once a month may well have problems of commitment from his team. His other choice, of course, is not to collect the anger stamp in the first place, but rather to talk openly with his subordinates at (or as near as possible to) the time of their mistake, transgression or poor performance.

In another situation an employee may tolerate appalling treatment from his boss for years without a murmur, and then one day wreck a piece of machinery, when all his or her pent-up feelings eventually explode. Again, there is an alternative choice, that is the expression of feelings and needs by directly confronting the 'put downs' as they occur (or by changing job). One of the goals of TA is to help people give up existing stamp collections, deal with feelings, needs and wants as they occur and stop collecting stamps in the future.

REFERENCE

1 S. Woollams, M. Brown and K. Huige, *Transactional Analysis in Brief,* Huron Valley Institute, 1974.

9 Scripts

DEFINITION OF SCRIPTS

One of the most powerful ideas in transactional analysis is the concept of life script, first elaborated by Berne.[1] A life script is a personal plan decided on at an early age (four to seven years old) by each individual in response to external events. The most important external factor for an offspring is the behaviour, attitudes and influences of parents, or, in their absence, other authority figures. On the basis of this influence, we make decisions about what kind of person we are and what kind of life we are going to lead, these decisions being crucial to our well-being and 'survival' when we are young. The problem is that these decisions or adaptations we make at this time may be dysfunctional in our relationships with others when we are older. The powerful effect of parental messages is based on the situational constraints facing children. For example, they are very small when compared to parents; they do not have a fully formed Adult ego state to help them understand what is going on, and in any case are often not given much information about events, or are given distorted information; and last of all, they have no choice to leave and find a better place to live!

The concept of scripts was foreshadowed to some extent by Adler[2] and his idea of life goals. Both Adler and transactional analysis confront the notion that we are entirely autonomous beings, but propose that most of us have to work for autonomy (the freedom to make our own choices and decisions) in the face of 'archaic' (i.e. early) influences. The more rigid the script, the more difficult it is to achieve this autonomy.

SCRIPT DECISIONS

Using structural analysis as a basis (see Chapter 2), the formation of scripts probably occurs according to the sequence of decisions shown in Figure 9.1. Firstly C_1 experiences and reacts at a feeling level to the grown-ups' behaviour, attitudes and messages (verbal and non-verbal). Under this exposure, A_1 (Little Professor) employs creativity to plan the best way to gain acceptance and recognition, avoid rejection and gain strokes, whether positive or negative, conditional or unconditional. P_1 then carries out this plan. This 'decision' is effective

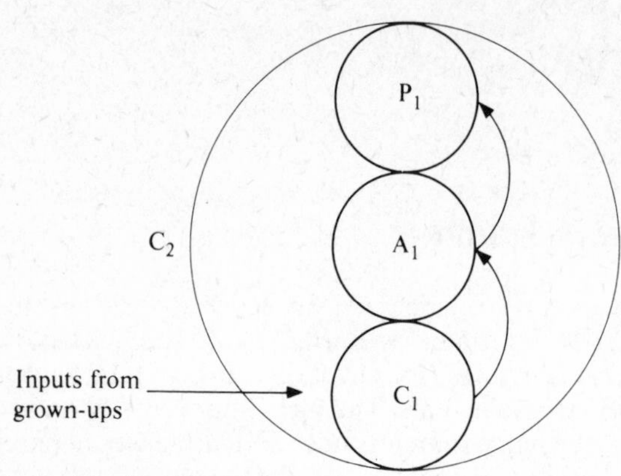

Figure 9.1 Script decisions

at the time, but later (in adulthood) it may prove to be a barrier to effective relationships and a fulfilling life.

PHASES IN SCRIPT DEVELOPMENT

The early phases in the development of a script proceed approximately as follows.[3]

0–6 MONTHS OLD

Our primary transaction with the environment is through crying, feeding and physical stroking. Through these transactions we conclude what sort of world we live in – scarey or happy, friendly or hostile.

6–18 MONTHS OLD

This phase is characterised by exploration of our environment (our physical mobility increases dramatically over this time) through the development of our 'Little Professor' capacity. If our needs to explore are blocked at this stage, it may influence our capacity for spontaneity, creativity and motivation later. At this stage, we begin deciding our self-worth in relation to others, i.e. our life position (see Chapter 5). In addition, through conditioned stroking, we may learn certain behaviours as major options for life, e.g. being stupid or being strong.

18 MONTHS–3 YEARS

This period marks the development of the Adult ego state; we are learning how to think and how to remember. We also make decisions about control issues – whether to be compliant or rebellious, dependent or independent.

3–6 YEARS OLD

This period is characterised by magical thinking ('If I think certain thoughts, certain things will automatically happen') and fantasising. The crucial decision is made about 'What happens to someone like me?' The model chosen may well be a member of the family (successful father, blacksheep uncle). Sometimes the model has a similarity to a fairy story (e.g. Sleeping Beauty, waiting for her prince) or a comic hero (e.g. Dan Dare, leading an adventurous life, destroying evil).

THE SCRIPT MATRIX

The script matrix, developed by Berne[1] gives a transactional view of script formation and is illustrated in Figure 9.2. The transactions indicated by *a, b, c* and *d* can be differentiated in terms of their consequences, as follows.

INJUNCTIONS, ATTRIBUTIONS AND IDENTIFICATIONS (*a* in Figure 9.2)

Injunctions arise in P_1 of the grown-up. They are frequently transmitted non-verbally and the 'giver' often denies giving them. They are heavily grounded in feelings and hence not easily defined, let alone challenged. They are usually repeated and have varying degrees of severity. They can be:

1 Low-level socially acceptable, referred to as first degree injunctions. For example, a child picking up food from the floor and eating it would probably at least get scowled at, if not told, 'Don't do that'
2 Devious and crooked, and perhaps backed-up by blackmail (second degree). For example, 'If you want some sweets, don't tell your father I broke his watch'
3 Very threatening, backed up by raging and screaming and even physical violence (third degree). For example, 'Don't do that or I'll kill you!'

Injunctions are limiting and constraining in their effect, and may require effort on our part to become aware of them. They are frequently a reflection of the parent(s)' own unresolved issues left over

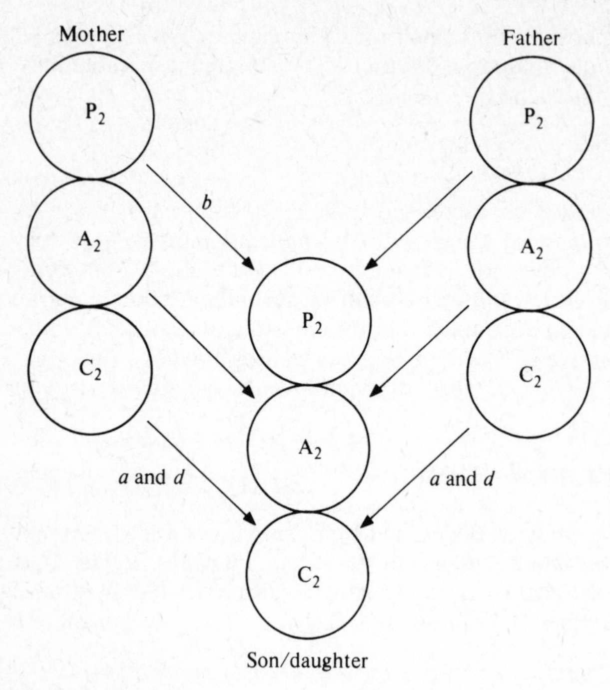

Figure 9.2 Script matrix

from his/her childhood.

Attributions also come from P_1 in the grown-up. They are parental definitions of who we are (e.g. 'You are . . . pretty, clever, good, naughty, a nuisance, crazy, stupid, etc.') and, as the examples show, may be socially positive or negative. One way to get in touch with our attributions is to focus on how our mother and father would describe us.

Identifications also arise from P_1 and are parental definitions of who we are like, e.g. 'You're just like you father, Uncle Joe, etc. . . .' (who was a great success, or who drank himself to death).

Depending on the degree of repetition and severity of the injunctions, attributions and identifications, children make decisions about what kind of person they are and how they are going to lead their life (e.g. 'Ah! so I'm like my Uncle Joe, who drinks a lot . . .').

PRESCRIPTIONS (*b* in Figure 9.2)

These are less potent in script formation than injunctions, etc. and come from P_2 of the grown-up. They are concerned with moral judgements and values and with social behaviour and standards, generally beginning at a later age, when the individual is more competent to deal with them. These messages often form the basis of a secondary script, referred to as the counterscript. They may be in opposition to the injunctions, or congruent with them.[4] For example a 'be independent' counterscript message will reinforce a 'don't be close' injunction. Similarly a 'work hard' counterscript message will reinforce a 'don't feel' injunction, a situation very common in men. Unlike many injunctions, prescriptions are socially acceptable and are statements that parents are willing to tell their friends or relatives about. For example:

'We always told him to work hard if he wanted to get on in life.'
'We always brought her up to help around the house, so she would make someone a good wife.'

They are verbal, conscious and overt.

Where prescriptions oppose injunctions, an individual sometimes suddenly shows a radical change in behaviour which may be socially judged as 'improvement'. What may actually be occurring is a switch from basic script to counterscript, and true autonomy is therefore not actually achieved. The change may be very temporary, as, for example, some alcoholics who reform and then relapse into drinking again.

PROGRAMME (PATTERN) (*c* in Figure 9.2)

This comes from the Adult in the parent of the same sex and is a demonstration of how injunctions, attributions and counterscript messages can be carried out. For example, a mother to daughter 'here's how to use make-up' programme (perhaps reinforced by a father to daughter 'be beautiful' prescription).

PROVOCATION ('LITTLE DEMON') (*d* in Figure 9.2)

Some children receive crazy messages from the grown-up's Child ego state, usually without the parent being aware of what they are doing. For example, 'Go on, have another accident, ha! ha!' or 'Go on, get into trouble, ha! ha!'. Such messages are the source of much misery and self-abuse later in life.

PERMISSIONS

For healthy development, each of us needs a series of 'permissions' to develop our capacities fully.[5] All too frequently this development is interfered with by injunctions acting in opposition to the permissions. These permissions are listed below, starting with the most important.

TO EXIST

The basic permission anyone needs is to exist, by being cared for, loved and stroked (see Chapter 3). A surprising number of children don't receive this permission and hence get 'don't exist' injunctions instead. They may be neglected, ignored and continually told: 'Don't bother me!' 'Get out of the way!' 'You're a nuisance!' In adulthood they may carry this through to killing themselves, by suicide, alcoholism, drug addiction or even overwork.

TO FEEL SENSATIONS

The ability to feel hunger and thirst, hot and cold, pressure and pain is vital for survival. However, some children get their responses to these sensations discounted when they are young. For example, they may grow up without an awareness of hunger, as in some forms of schizophrenia. Some men grow up with a low awareness of pain, because of early injunctions such as 'Don't cry!' backed up by culturally supported prescriptions such as, 'Be a man!'; 'Be strong!'; 'Grit your teeth!'

TO FEEL FEELINGS

The four basic reactive feelings – sad, mad (in the sense of angry), glad and scared – are available to all of us at birth. However, if they are discounted in our family situation, we may choose not to express them and instead learn to feel only what other people want us to (racket feelings, Chapter 8). There are some important sex differences in this respect in our society. Many men get 'don't be scared' injunctions, but get permission to be angry, whereas many women get 'don't be angry' injunctions, but get permission to be scared.

Even if we get permission to feel certain feelings, we may not get permission to express them openly. This block is supported quite widely in our organisations where there are often strong taboos against demonstrating feelings. The trouble is that feelings felt but not expressed 'rumble' around and get in the way of work. They may be collected and 'cashed in' at a later date (see Chapter 8), or even contribute to illness (e.g. headaches, back pain, ulcers).

TO THINK

While there may well be an important genetic influence on our intellectual capacities, parental influences are also a key determinant. Some children get ample permission to think both from parental example and parental support in reading, solving problems and progress at school. Others ignore this aspect of their children's development and even give messages to discourage or block the growth of thinking capacities, e.g. 'You're a stupid boy!'; 'You've got no idea have you!'

TO BE CLOSE TO OTHERS

Some parents are warm and affectionate to one another and to their children, giving them permission to be close to others when they grow up. Other families shun physical contact and displays of feelings of closeness and hence give 'don't be close' messages. Many fathers give their sons 'don't be close' messages by working long hours or travelling extensively, and their sons grow up to be managers or professionals in the same mould – making decisions and money instead of close contact with others.

TO BE THE SEX YOU ARE

A minority of people get confused messages about whether they are a boy or a girl, leading to considerable misery when they are grown up.

TO BE THE AGE YOU ARE

Some children get the injunction 'don't grow up' and remain mummy's little darling for the rest of their lives; sometimes they appear to be very childish. In some families, the parents can't wait for the kids to get out of nappies, get off the potty, get off to school, grow-up and get out of their lives. The children may well overhear messages like, 'She's advanced for her age' or 'He's a serious little boy, very grown up in some ways', which may lead to the offspring abandoning their childhood before time and losing contact with their Free Child.

TO 'MAKE IT'

Finally, some children get a 'don't make it' message loud and clear, e.g. 'He's useless' or 'He'll never come to anything'. This message may be about life generally, or more specific – about work, sex or happiness. Very often, the message is based on parents' jealousy at the thought of the child's being more successful than them.

CLASSIFICATION OF SCRIPTS

On the basis of the kinds of injunctions given and the quality of the script outcomes involved, scripts can be illustrated and classified in several ways, for example:

WINNERS, NON-WINNERS AND LOSERS

This way of classifying scripts is based on the stroke balance that we establish for ourselves in our early years (Chapter 3).

A winner has a script that produces mostly positive strokes. A winner is happy most of the time and fulfils his or her potential, whether as a housewife, doctor, businessman or dustman. They have problems like everyone, but deal with them effectively and constructively. Winners learn from their experiences without punishing themselves with their Critical Parent. They have fun without hurting themselves or others, i.e. they have plenty of Free Child. They take care of the present and the future with equal effectiveness. Non-winners often get jealous and annoyed with them, because they don't seem to have so many problems.

Most of us are non-winners. A non-winner experiences an even distribution of positive and negative strokes, usually not highly charged. Examples are the hardworking business man who uses his Adult a lot, but avoids intimacy, and the hard-working housewife who does not use her Adult much, except to run the house, but her Nurturing Parent a great deal of look after her family. They have their ups and downs, their good times and bad times. They are 'successful' in life compared with the losers, and yet still don't experience all the joy to be had.

The loser experiences mostly negative strokes (through physical or mental illness, family break-up, breaking the law, etc.) and often gets involved with the police, lawyers, solicitors, probation officers, prison officers, social workers, therapists, doctors and counsellors. If they find their way into business organisations they eventually get kicked out for fiddling the till, taking to the bottle or failing to perform.

NO LOVE, NO MIND, NO JOY SCRIPTS[4]

This classification of (non-winner and loser) scripts is based on some essential ingredients to a full life – to have love, to have a mind and to have joy.

A 'no love' script is based on injunctions limiting stroke options, referred to as the stroke economy (Chapter 3):

don't give strokes if you have them to give
don't ask for strokes when you need them
don't accept strokes if you want them
don't reject strokes when you don't want them
don't give yourself strokes.

It seems to affect women more than men and leads to feelings of being unloved and/or depression. In extreme cases it may lead to suicide or catatonia.

A 'no mind' script is based on discounts of a child's intuition, emotions and rational thinking capacities. Since intuition, feelings and thinking are all important in different ways to getting on with life, people with 'no mind' scripts have problems coping, and may ultimately become insane.

A 'no joy' script is based on injunctions preventing people from experiencing their bodies and thus encouraging them to disregard their bodily sensations, pleasant or unpleasant. Consequently, bodies and feelings are split off from 'self'. It leads to over-dependence on 'intellect' and rationality and may lead to dependence on medication, nicotine, alcohol and drugs.

SCRIPTS AND TRANSACTIONAL ANALYSIS

The ways we give and get our strokes, structure our time, indulge in rackets, collect stamps, and play games will depend on our preferred life position and the script we adopt. Our games, rackets and stamps, and time-structuring choices are all part of our script reinforcing and motivating system. This inter-relationship is expressed generally and approximately in Figure 9.3.

Our early experiences give rise to decisions about ourselves, others and the world. This gives rise to the adoption of a preferred life position and a stroke balance, leading to the adoption of a script and script reinforcing behaviour and followed by some kind of script 'pay-off' in adulthood, which may be dramatic or mundane, successful or disastrous. Certainly a relationship can be seen between script messages and games (Figure 9.4).

Script theory is one of the most important ideas to come out of transactional analysis. More work has yet to be done on elaborating the idea and there are certainly one or two aspects unresolved. For example, the internal processes in each individual are vital. Somebody can have a 'bad' upbringing and still turn out 'good', i.e. have a winner script. So there is a distinction to be made between the message which is sent, the way it is received and the decision or adaptation made.

Figure 9.3 Script development

Early experiences	*Decisions*	*Adoption of preferred life position and stroke balance*	*Adoption of a script*	*Plus*	*Script reinforcing behaviour*	*Script payoff*
Some verbal, some non-verbal, some direct, some indirect →	About self, others and the world →	Answering the question 'what sort of person am I?' →	Answering the question 'what happens to someone like me?' (e.g. winner, non-winner, loser)		Games Rackets Stamps Time structuring	For example: Achieving great things Being alone Going mad Committing suicide Leading an ordinary life
Permissions						
Injunctions						
Attributions						
Identifications						
Counterscript messages						
Come-ons						
Patterns						

Figure 9.4 Some script messages and related games

Script message	*Game*
You can't trust anyone!	Now I've got you, you son of a bitch
Don't be satisfied with yourself	Harried
Don't think!	Stupid

IMPLICATIONS FOR ORGANISATIONS AND TRAINERS

In terms of application to date, script theory has been almost entirely the province of the therapist. One major exception to this is the application of the idea of organisational scripts, discussed in the next section. Individual script theory has proved to be a major vehicle for therapy and personal growth, with the development of life script questionnaires and also techniques to help people to regress to early times in their life and consequently 're-decide' their behaviour and change self-limiting or destructive adaptations.

Nevertheless, it is an important area of theory for a number of reasons. First, it offers a significant 'bridge' between personality and interpersonal behaviour on the one hand, and the behaviour and norms of groups, organisations and whole societies on the other. The Whites have started to explore this issue in their work on cultural scripting.[6]

Second, it raises some pertinent issues for organisations concerning organisational change. For example, recent legislation in both the UK and USA has, in theory, removed barriers to the recruitment, remuneration and development of women at work. However, any amount of legislation is unlikely to produce more than compliance from men with a lifetime of contamination about sex roles, and will not of itself change the scripts of women. Much female scripting itself limits the opportunity of women for advancement and development in organisations. For example, many jobs demand highly developed skills of logic, reasoning and numeracy, all Adult ego state functions. However in many families, this capacity is discounted in women, and consequently our percentage of female engineers, for example, though rising, is still small. In order to overcome such problems, some kind of planned educational programme is required in organisations, to reduce prejudice in men and help women make new decisions about their capabilities.

Third, script theory offers help on some important individual problems in organisations. For example, TA views alcoholism not as a disease but rather as a third degree game that constitutes a serious and damaging script (loser or 'no joy') This idea has been put to work with alcoholics with some measure of success; i.e. alcoholics have been fully cured and their loser script changed so that they are able to imbibe socially without getting addicted again.[7]

Another important application has been to use script theory to examine the decline of motivation amongst managers in their middle years. In Western society many men have 'achiever scripts' based on conditional stroking for success and attainment, very often at the expense of satisfactory relationships with others. In many cases, there is a fall-off of motivation in middle years amongst managers, resulting in the organisation carrying 'deadwood'. Novey[8] suggests ways of dealing with this, using TA, and a summary of this work is given in Chapter 18.

ORGANISATIONAL SCRIPTS

It is possible to apply the ideas of individual script theory to organisations, at least to a limited extent. This is not to say that organisations behave like individuals, but rather that there are some parallels, in terms of both the script matrix idea and types of scripts. However, particularly when considering small family-based organisations, there may be close identification of family script and organisational script; a point worth noting by those advising and consulting small firms.

SCRIPT MATRIX – INJUNCTIONS, PERMISSIONS AND PRESCRIPTIONS IN ORGANISATIONS

In terms of 'survival' in the organisational 'family' any new employee has to discover the 'dos and don'ts' or organisational permissions and injunctions in his new place of employment. Quite what the individual does in response to these discoveries will depend on his or her individual script and script reinforcing behaviour (games, etc.). From an organisational viewpoint, there are two important dimensions involved, namely authority and formality.

As far as authority is concerned, the more authoritarian an organisation is, the more Critical Parent it will be in its behaviour. As a consequence the more frequent and heavy the injunctions are likely to be, such as

'You're not paid to think, you're paid to do what you're told! (don't think)
'You're here to work, get on with it and stop talking' (don't be close)

Such injunctions may be underpinned by a basic set of attributions, e.g.

'You (the workers) are lazy, stupid, irresponsible, destructive, disloyal, tardy, etc. . . .'. Conversely, the more participative and collaborative the organisation, the greater the emphasis on Adult–Adult and Free Child–Free Child transactions, and the greater the permission for staff to develop, learn, explore and innovate. The likely outcome of this is a greater organisational capacity to survive and grow. This is not to say that there is no place for Critical Parent behaviour, for example, in enforcing safety regulations.

As some organisations have found, however, changing to a participative style of organisation can be difficult, and even disastrous, if adequate structures, help and time aren't allowed for all concerned to relearn and cope with the change. All parties involved require help in giving up the Critical Parent–Adapted Child relationships they are used to in favour of more Adult–Adult relationships.

As far as formality is concerned, some injunctions ('don'ts') are elaborated in various documents, for example:

terms and conditions of employment (these are of course heavily influenced by governmental injunctions)
employee handbooks
house journals and newsletters
induction course notes.

Others are informal, that is they are an established part of the organisation's culture, but are not explicitly documented. Discovering them can be a difficult and sometimes traumatic experience for new employees.

As well as the injunctions and permissions, new employees are confronted with the organisation's prescriptions. These again may be explicit slogans and exhortations, displayed on notice boards and in house journals, or may be more covert and insidious ('I'd like a quiet word with you. You see, in order to get on around here, you have to be . . .').

Organisational injunctions and prescriptions are frequently embedded in precedence – 'the way we've always done things' – and they have a close parallel to family traditions. The greater the power of precedence, the more rigid and stifling the organisational script is likely to be. This gives us a way of beginning to diagnose organisational scripts. Another clue is the presence, or absence, of photographs of key figures (present and previous chairmen, for example), particularly if it is a family firm or is strongly influenced by a particular family or a charismatic and controlling figure. One way the 'ghosts' of founding families can haunt organisations is through passing on script messages.

TYPES OF SCRIPTS IN ORGANISATIONS[9]

Some organisations can be viewed as having 'going somewhere fast' scripts, based on high achievement and motivation, with rapid exploitation of market opportunities and successful innovation of new techniques, approaches and products. Other organisations have 'ticking over steadily' scripts, doing the minimum required to keep their share of the market or maintain the service they purport to be providing. Some have 'going downhill slowly' scripts, with fortunes that are diminishing year by year and a top management team living on the glories of the past. Some small firms have 'self-destruct' scripts where the founder-owner keeps all the responsibility, rarely delegates and may even keep technical 'secrets' to himself. On his death, no one is equipped managerially or technically to carry the business on and so the dole queue grows longer. In 'sudden crisis' scripts an organisation appears to encounter a major and unexpected crisis from nowhere, with redundancies and financial collapse, possibly being rescued by outside intervention. As with an individual whose script has a nervous breakdown as an outcome, for example, there are frequently indicators of the trauma to come in 'sudden crisis' scripts, for those perceptive enough to see them. In those organisations living in the past, considerable energy is spent in maintaining the organisation's script. Critical Parent behaviour is aimed at preserving corporate sacred cows and dictating standards that are often irrelevant to such issues as productivity, efficiency and safety. All too easily this hooks rebellious behaviour in the Adapted Child of employees, with consequent loss of work effectiveness.

REFERENCES

1 E. Berne, *What Do You Say After You Say Hello?* Grove Press Inc., 1972; Corgi, 1975.
2 J. Simonceaux, 'Adlerian psychology and TA' in *Techniques in Transactional Analysis,* Muriel James et al., Addison-Wesley, 1977.
3 P. Levin, *Becoming the Way We Are. A Transactional Guide to Personal Development,* Group House, Berkeley, 1974.
4 C. Steiner, *Scripts People Live,* Grove Press Inc., 1974; Bantam Books, 1975.
5 J. Allen and B. Allen, 'Scripts: The Role of Permission', *Transactional Analysis Journal,* vol. 2, no. 2, April 1972.

6 T. and J.D. White, 'The implications of cultural scripting' in *Transactional Analysis after Eric Berne,* Graham Barnes et al., Harper's College Press, 1977.
7 C. Steiner, *Games Alcoholics Play*, Grove Press Inc., 1971.
8 T. Novey, *TA for Management,* Jalmar Press Inc., 1974.
9 D. Jongeward et al., *Everybody Wins,* Addison-Wesley, 1973.

10 TA and other approaches to psychology

The aim of this chapter is to 'put things in context', by relating TA to the three important approaches to psychology today, i.e. psychoanalysis, behaviourism and humanistic psychology. TA has characteristics in common with all three. This comparison is at least partially personal and may well not reflect the views of others.

TA AND PSYCHOANALYSIS

It is appropriate to consider psychoanalysis first, because this was Berne's own theoretical background (see Chapter 1). The term 'ego states' means states or aspects of the ego experienced phenomenologically on a day-to-day basis (see Chapter 2). Many of the characteristics of the Parent seem similar to those of the superego, and those of the Child similar to the id.

However, TA has developed considerably and its technology and practices, as well as the theory base, are very different from its psychoanalytic origins. Thus id, ego and superego are very much inferred categories,[1] whereas ego states by definition are groups of observable behaviours. Some distinctions are highlighted in Figure 10.1.

Figure 10.1 Some comparative aspects of id and Child, superego and Parent

Freudian concepts	*Bernian concepts*
Id – no external programming – unconscious – negative connotations	Child – partly externally programmed (Adapted Child) – without awareness – positive connotations, as well as negative
Superego – limiting, controlling, 'conscience'	Parent – caring aspect (Nurturing Parent) as well as limiting (Critical Parent)

Psychoanalysis is very much concerned with the 'unconscious' and with dreams, whereas TA strives to bring things into awareness from the 'pre-conscious', the things that are there outside our awareness.

Psychoanalysis originally was very concerned with individual behaviour in the form of intrapsychic events. While not neglecting this area altogether, TA is concerned primarily with interpsychic events, i.e. behaviour between people, and offers a potent approach to looking at and developing awareness and skills in interpersonal communication. It is true to say that some post-Freudian psychoanalysts have concerned themselves more with interpersonal behaviour, e.g. Karen Horney[2] and, more recently, John Southgate and his colleagues.[3]

Lastly, psychoanalysis may well be of more limited use than TA in the development of people, their potential and relationships, in organisations, because of the psychoanalyst's focus on the abnormal (TA embraces the normal and the abnormal). Perhaps one exception to this has been indirectly, through the development of the Tavistock approach to learning about leadership, authority and group behaviour. One of the key influences on this approach is the work of Wilfred Bion who, like Berne, had a strong psychoanalytical background.[4] But TA still has some common ground with psychoanalysis. Both are, after all, analytic approaches to the problem areas of individual and human experience, and, unfortunately, some TA therapists use the medical model of man (i.e. man the 'sick' animal) in practice at least, if not in theory. Both approaches view early experiences as fundamental to later behaviour. Perhaps this is where the similarity ends however. TA is infinitely optimistic in that, despite these early years, we have the capacity later to make fresh choices and change our behaviour to obtain more effective relationships and happier lives. Freud was never so optimistic.

TA AND BEHAVIOURISM

Together with psychoanalysis, behaviourism has become a major accepted 'establishment' approach to human psychology, based on the work of such pioneers as Thorndyke, Watson and Skinner.[5] Not only has it had an impact on therapy through such people as Wolpe[6] it has also had a sizeable impact on organisations. For example, Skinner has used behaviourism as a vehicle for organisation development. Behaviourism has influenced training in organisations directly, through such notions as terminal objectives, and through the development of that whole branch of training called 'programmed learning'.

The distinctive core of behaviourism is its use of the scientific approach applied to examining and explaining human behaviour. For example:

> events and phenomena are related by cause and effect
> the observer is separate from the observed, without mutual influence.

The key elements of behaviourism are:

> 1 Identification of the basic units and laws of human behaviour, often by extrapolation from experiments with animals
> 2 The development from these laws of a comprehensive abstract model for understanding and predicting human behaviour. The behaviourist is thus concerned with the regularities in man such as drives, reflexes, habits and conditioned responses, and is interested in demonstrating that any new experience is merely a variant on simpler and already established phenomena.

As a consequence, behaviourism seeks to establish what is average and normal behaviour, rather than individual, exceptional and idiosyncratic.

TA shares some features with behaviourism. Both are analytical, attempting to classify human responses and behaviour and to relate cause and effect. Behaviourism is firmly embedded in classical scientific thought, and Berne was always very concerned to be scientific. There has always been an interest in TA circles to experimentally verify the models used. However, TA is much more explicit and self-defining, in comparison with behaviourism, and does not follow classical scientific groundrules so closely. Certainly, the assumption in behaviourism that the observer is separate from the observed, is not held in TA; for example, ego state diagnosis is by both 'objective' observation of the behaviour witnessed *and* subjective experience (see Chapter 2).

The concept of 'contract' used by TA therapists has much in common with the reward/punishment schedule used in Skinner's operant conditioning approach.[5] Operant conditioning (or shaping theory) proposes that rewards can be used to elicit desirable behaviour, and punishments to extinguish undesirable. This model can be readily demonstrated with rats and pigeons, and 'extended' to humans. However, it raises ethical issues concerning who defines what is desirable and undesirable behaviour, who administers what punishment, the quality of the 'shaped' behaviour, and other issues of power, responsibility and free will.

After a period of settling into a TA therapy group, a client is expected to explore problem areas with a therapist and ultimately to establish a behaviour goal or 'contract' in terms of what he or she will stop doing and start doing 'from now on'. When a client has agreed to a contract, the therapist and the rest of the group will reward, support and positively stroke evidence of changed behaviour towards the goal. If the client fails to meet the contract, the therapist will 'punish' the client in some way, even to the extent of excluding the individual from the group.

TA differs from behaviourism in two key respects:

1 By using a model and language that are deliberately intended for sharing between professional and client, thereby bridging the gap between observer and observed, a gap that is an integral part not only of behaviourism but also of psychoanalysis
2 TA is paradoxically concerned not only with analysis and the consequent reduction of behaviour into components, but also with change, growth and development of individuals to become 'more whole' and realise more fully their potential. This is embodied is such concepts as Free Child, Adult and Nurturing Parent, and more particularly scripts and autonomy, and also in the striving for new choices in behaviour. The particular importance of the concept of autonomy will be referred to in Chapter 11.

In these two differences from behaviourism, TA is more closely aligned to the ethos of humanistic psychology.

HUMANISTIC PSYCHOLOGY

Since the Second World War an important new approach has developed in psychology, not yet fully accepted or established academically. This approach, humanistic psychology[7] is sometimes referred to as the human potential movement or third force psychology. It is practically expressed in a collection of different techniques[8] (e.g. Gestalt therapy, encounter groups, psychodrama, bio-energetics, co-counselling, client-centred counselling, meditation). The approach is influenced by Western humanism and existentialism, and also Eastern philosophies, with some common assumptions and values, as follows:

1 In general, people are seen as normally using only a fraction of their innate capacities and creativity, with a potential for experience and activity as yet not realised. The varying techniques of humanistic psychology are ways of releasing this potential
2 The reductionism of behaviourism and its 'nothing but' model of human beings is rejected, and experimentation with

animals seen as giving at best partial data on the nature of man and probably misleading in many instances. Classical 'Newtonian' scientific methodology is limited and limiting in the understanding of human behaviour, and humanistic psychology seeks to examine the subjective, the individual, the exceptional and the unpredicted as well as the regular, average and normal
3 Humanistic psychology is concerned to continuously describe human experience rather than give an ultimate analysis of it.

Whilst largely American in origin, it has had a significant impact on Western Europe. Organisationally, it has had a considerable effect on the areas of motivation, training and organisation development. For example, many human aspects courses for managers feature the work of Maslow (one of the leading 'gurus' of the movement) with his 'hierarchy of needs' [9] and of McGregor with his 'theory X and theory Y' model of management style.[10] The T-group[11] with its origins in the group dynamics of Lewin and colleagues and its distinctly human potential and growth theme, has made a controversial impact on human relations training. The T-group in turn had a substantial impact on what was to become known as 'organisation development'. Other humanistic psychology approaches have had a lesser impact, partly because of the unacceptability of some of their technology in male-dominated environments (e.g. the extensive body contact involved in the Schutz-type open encounter group.)[12] However, gestalt therapy, which is often used by TA therapists as an adjunct to their work, is now beginning to be applied in organisations as a novel approach to human relations training.[13]

While TA is different from most humanistic psychology approaches because of its more extensive use of theoretical models, it does show a common emphasis on the growth and fulfilment of the individual.

TA endorses the values of authenticity, personal power, self-understanding and personal change, values firmly rooted in humanistic psychology, and taboo in repressive cultures because of their consequences for leadership and authority. Through the concept of the Parent, Berne explores authority and leadership issues more extensively than some other approaches. As in planned organisation development, the emphasis is evolutionary, not revolutionary (see Chapter 15).

In summary; the concepts of TA owe much to psychoanalysis; there is a limited technological affinity with behaviourism; and the inherent and expressed values are akin to those in humanistic psychology. It is the question of values that is probably most important, since any model or theory can be made to work or 'proved right'. The central value of TA is personal responsibility, in other words:

> I am responsible for my own actions and behaviour with an awareness of the consequences for others.

REFERENCES

1 R.C. Drye, 'Psychoanalysis and TA' in *Techniques in TA,* Muriel James et al., Addison-Wesley, 1977.
2 K. Horney, *Self Analysis,* Norton, 1942.
3 J. Southgate and R. Randall, *The Barefoot Psychoanalyst,* The Association of Karen Horney Psychoanalytic Counsellors, 1976.
4 W.R. Bion *Experiences in Groups,* Tavistock Publications, 1961.
5 See A. Neel, *Theories of Personality,* University of London Press, 1971.
6 J. Wolpe, 'The practice of behaviour therapy' in *Human Development*, Selected Readings, M. and N. Haimowitz (eds), T.Y. Cromwell, 1973.
7 J.F.T. Bugental, *Challenges of Humanistic Psychology,* McGraw-Hill Inc., 1967.
8 J. Rowan, *Ordinary Ecstasy: Humanistic Psychology in Action,* Routledge and Kegan Paul Ltd., 1976.
9 A.H. Maslow, *Motivation and Personality,* Harper and Row, 1954.
10 D. McGregor, *The Human Side of Enterprise,* McGraw-Hill Inc., 1960.
11 L.P. Bradford, J.R. Gibb and K.D. Benne, *T-Group Theory and Laboratory Method,* John Wiley and Sons, 1964.
12 W.C. Schutz, *Joy: Expanding Human Awareness,* Souvenir Press Ltd., 1971.
13 S.H. Herman and M. Korenich, *Authentic Management: A Gestalt Approach to Organisations and their Development,* Addison-Wesley, 1977.

Part II
Using TA

11 The goals of TA and its application in training

THE MAIN CONCEPTS OF TA

It may be useful at this point to remind the reader of the key concepts of TA and their relationships, in a summary form (Figure 11.1).

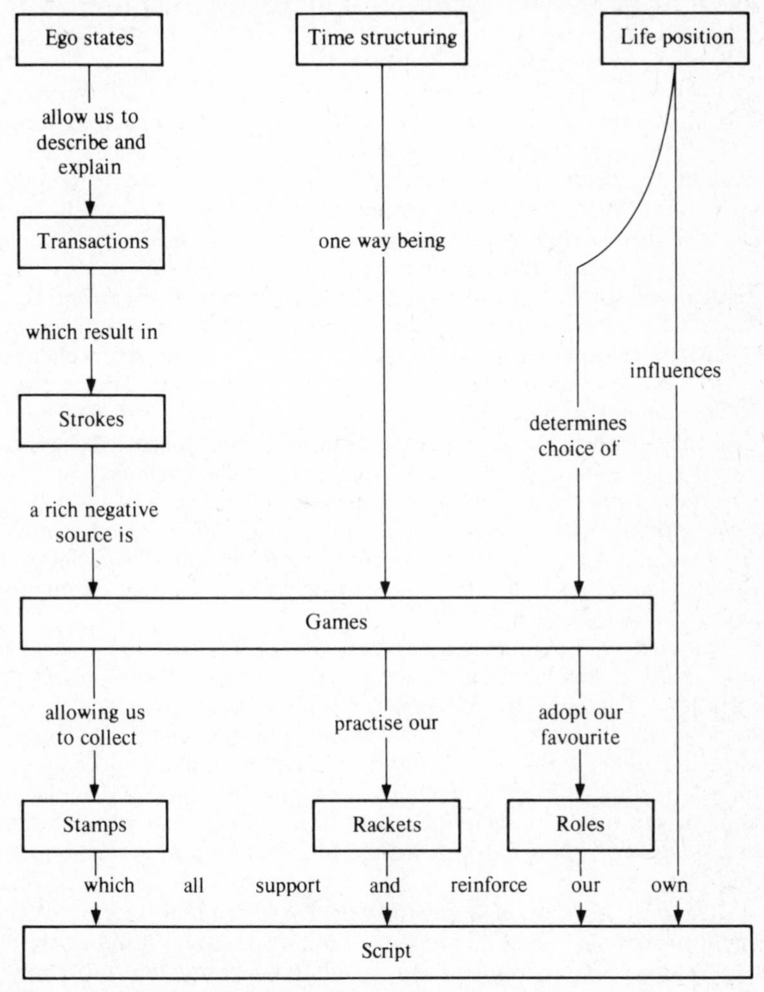

Figure 11.1 The main concepts of TA

AUTONOMY AS THE GOAL OF TA

In *Games People Play,* Berne states his view that the goal of TA is the achievement of personal autonomy. By autonomy we mean:

personal self-government
the freedom to make our own choices and decisions about our own lives, without manipulation or exploitation by others
the right to assert and say what we want without resorting to active aggression
freedom from putting ourselves down.

Two important riders need to be added. First, that our choices are informed choices and we have the maximum of information and feedback from others on the possible consequences of our intended behaviours. Second, that autonomy does not involve denying our responsibility to others, particularly by causing physical hurt.

This goal recurs throughout humanistic psychology. It also has implications for the distribution and use of power in organisations. Thus if an organisation chose to develop increased autonomy amongst its staff, there would be a considerable demand on its managers changing to a more open style of management, for example. This in turn would demand a major planned organisation change effort. There would also be the wider issues of the cultural support for such a change, and its congruence with the economic goals of the organisation.

Berne considered that autonomy consists of three capacities. One of them, intimacy (the capacity for openness with others in close non-gamey relationships), has been referred to in Chapter 6. The other two aspects, awareness and spontaneity, need to be examined closely as each has a paradoxical quality.

Awareness is the capacity to see the world as it is, with the 'eyes of a child', without any labels, expectations, preconditioning or passed-on attitudes. This means having a non-interpretative and non-judgemental contact with the world of things and others. It also means being in contact with our own internal world, with mind and body in unison, feeling and experiencing everything for ourselves without being driven by the past. In other words, awareness is existing in the 'here-and-now', being in touch with how we feel and what our 'wants' are.

The paradox is that, in seeing the world in such a non-interpretative way, transactional analysts are using an interpretative framework to achieve this goal, i.e. using interpretation to take away interpretation.

Berne's specific use of the word 'spontaneity' produces particular difficulties to TA initiates at first. By 'spontaneous', Berne meant the freedom to respond and interact from any of the three ego states, i.e. to have potential access to all these ego states in a given moment, selecting what is constructive, rejecting what is destructive. Now, spontaneous is usually taken to mean free unthinking instantaneous expression. This contradicts the TA use of the word, particularly when it is considered against another TA 'aim' – that of 'putting the Adult into the executive', i.e. using the Adult ego state to check internal and external data before interacting. This is hardly an instantaneous or unthinking process.

The use of the word spontaneity is perhaps better understood if looked at from a point of view of human development. As can be seen from Chapter 9 on scripts, early influences often cut down our choices to take advantage of all our capacities. In this sense, we lose our spontaneity, and parental influences reduce our range of responses, even limiting us to the same old repetitive dysfunctional ways (e.g. games and rackets) in given situations. It is in this sense, by lifting these parental embargos and giving back the personal power to grow and change with any situation, that TA seeks to recover our original childhood spontaneity.

THE GOALS OF TA IN TA TERMS

It is possible to make a general statement about those goals of TA that might be appropriate to organisations and their members, in TA terms. Taking each of the main theory areas of TA, in turn:

1 *Ego states*
Reduce dysfunctional Parent and Adapted Child behaviour
Develop an effective balance between the resources of the three ego states
Increase access to Natural Child creativity
Reduce/remove contamination

2 *Strokes*
Increase exchange of authentic, positive strokes and decrease inauthentic positive strokes and negative strokes
Break the stroke economy

3 *Transactions*
Increase the awareness of the consequences of different kinds of

transactions in interpersonal communication

4 *Life positions*
Increase the time spent in I+ U+ position as opposed to the other three life positions

5 *Time structuring*
Spend more time in intimacy
Increase or reduce the time spent in activities as appropriate
Increase skills in pastiming (in certain situations)

6 *Games*
Reduce the extent of games, particularly the harder ones
Avoid taking positions on the drama triangle

7 *Stamps*
Reduce stamp collecting and replace with more effective management of feelings

8 *Rackets*
Replace racket feelings with reactive feelings

9 *Life scripts*
Change from non-winner and loser scripts to winner scripts, at the personal and organisational level

Two important things need to be said here. First, some of these goals may not be achievable through training, but are rather the domain of therapy. Much depends on the individual concerned and the severity of the issue. The boundary between training and therapy will be looked at again later in the book. Second, most of the goals are phrased in terms of reduction (or increase); it is questionable whether dysfunctional behaviour can always be eradicated by an individual, with or without help from others. For example, conditions of severe personal stress for someone sometimes lead to a return to the bad old ways.

THE VALUES AND BELIEFS OF TA

Underlying the goals of TA are some important values and beliefs which any organisation needs to think about if using TA in a significant way. Are they congruent with the organisation's own view of the world and, if not, do they indicate directions in which the organisation wishes to develop? Some are listed here, though the list may by no means be exhaustive. Many of the assumptions are shared by other approaches.

IT IS POSSIBLE TO ANALYSE BEHAVIOUR IN A SYSTEM-

ATIC WAY

This is of course axiomatic for people using TA.

THE PAST INFLUENCES PRESENT BEHAVIOUR

In other words early childhood decisions, which may have been very functional at the time, will influence behaviour now and may or may not cause difficulties. By difficulties we mean the behaviour stemming from the decision in some way or other limits our capacities and choices for resolving problems, for self-development and for living fuller lives. This is not the same as saying that a person has to undergo therapy in order to overcome these difficulties. It is certainly a common concern in organisations that the introduction of TA heralds the 'digging up' of the past. However many issues can be resolved with the use of a well informed Adult and updated Parent in a training course.

WE CAN ALWAYS CHANGE

Our behaviour and even some of the central aspects of our personality can change. This demands, of course, our full investment and personal support and cooperation with the professional intervention of trainers, counsellors or therapists. However, whatever support we may get, the responsibility for change rests ultimately with ourselves. This value runs counter to some other schools of psychological thought such as some of the trait theorists (e.g. Eysenck).

THE QUALITY OF INTERPERSONAL RELATIONSHIPS INFLUENCES THE QUALITY OF ORGANISATIONAL AND CULTURAL LIFE

If we can improve the quality of relationships between people we can positively influence the health of our organisations and culture (e.g. more effectively manage conflict, manage deviant behaviour more humanely, reduce oppression, raise children more successfully, etc.).

MAN IS PROACTIVE, NOT REACTIVE

Put another way, rather than being the victims of destiny and other people's actions, we set ourselves up for situations, e.g. being overworked, putting up with the aggression of others, getting fired, being late for meetings and so on.

TAKE CARE OF YOURSELF

The most effective way I can look after you is to look after myself first. Then I can help you, instead of rescuing you.

WE ARE ULTIMATELY RESPONSIBLE FOR OUR OWN FEELINGS AND BEHAVIOUR

'You can't change me, only I can change me' seems sound enough to many people. However, the notion that other people can't make me behave in a specific way, rather I choose to behave in that way, seems to fly in the face of everyday experience. In addition, the fact that I choose my feelings (albeit, perhaps a stereotyped, racket feeling) goes against the cultural grain for many people. One of our favourite sayings is 'You make me feel – sad, angry, scared, etc.'. A more accurate statement is that one person can help or influence another into behaviour or feelings, but not positively make a specific feeling or behaviour happen. Very often when presented with the same situation, different individuals respond with different feelings and behaviour.

At the bottom of it all, the most important issue here is that if we assume others are responsible for our own behaviour and feelings, then we've given away our own personal power and control over our own destinies. If we assume the opposite, we're taking it back.

TRAINING AND EFFECTIVE RELATIONSHIPS BETWEEN PEOPLE

Before examining the question of the aims of TA in non-TA terms, two other questions need to be answered. First, what are 'effective' relationships between people; and second, what does training to develop such relationships (referred to by many names, including social skills, interpersonal skills, interpersonal relationships, interactive skill, human relationships training) purport to do?

As far as 'effective' or 'competent' relationships between people are concerned, Carby and Thakur[1] quote that '. . . "social competence" . . . involves:

> perceptual sensitivity – accurate perception of others
> warmth and rapport – affiliation, rapid response to others
> a repertoire of techniques
> flexibility
> energy and initiation – active people are more effective
> smooth response patterns – require long practice or training.'

Perception of others' behaviour and feelings seems to be an important skill in maintaining effective relationships. It is a variable skill in the population as a whole, and those low in this ability seem to induce demotivation and withdrawal or aggression in others. Both TA and other approaches are helpful in developing this skill. Of course, there are those who are *too* sensitive to others, and end up paying too much time and attention to others' needs, feelings and behaviours, instead of their own. Warmth and rapport in the sense of a general caring for (but not rescuing) others, together with mutual respect ('I'm OK, you're OK') and listening rather than answer-preparing and defending, are also key aspects of social competence and effective relationships. Having a repertoire of techniques and responses, and flexibility in their use, seem to mark effective relating to others, as opposed to relating in the same old programmed and stereotyped way. This is encapsulated in Berne's notion of spontaneity. Active, or pro-active, people are certainly more competent in the sense that they initiate, and get their needs and wants met, whilst being sensitive to their effect on other people. The ability to assert, however, seems to contradict smooth response patterns as a feature of effective relationships. This ability may well involve saying no and/or crossing transactions with a resultant break in the response patterns.

An important distinction to be made here is between assertion, which is the right to state and elaborate our own views and to take responsibility for their consequences, and aggression or hostility. These last two involve verbal (and physical) attacks on others, and generally taking away the self-worth of others. When we are asserting we say things like:

'I need to sort the problem out.'
'I want to be clear with you.'
but when we are hostile:
'You're an idiot.'
'The trouble with you is . . .'

As far as TA is concerned, two additions to the list are: first, authenticity, where people are 'straight' with one another on a basis of mutual respect and trust, as opposed to the use of manipulation and deception, and second, consciously looking at own and others' behaviour and its consequences, using such models as TA and supported by feedback. (This often seems to participants on courses a matter of making the implicit explicit, but an awareness of the concepts may contribute to increased personal power and effectiveness.)

The characteristics of low and high effectiveness in relationships are shown in Figure 11.2. Training for increased effectiveness in relationships and social competence (social skills training and the like) thus involves development along the dimensions shown in Figure 11.2, at least as far as TA is concerned. The next section looks at the aim of social skills training, not in TA terms nor in terms of the dimensions shown in Figure 11.2, but rather in more typical 'training terms'.

Figure 11.2 Dimensions of social competence

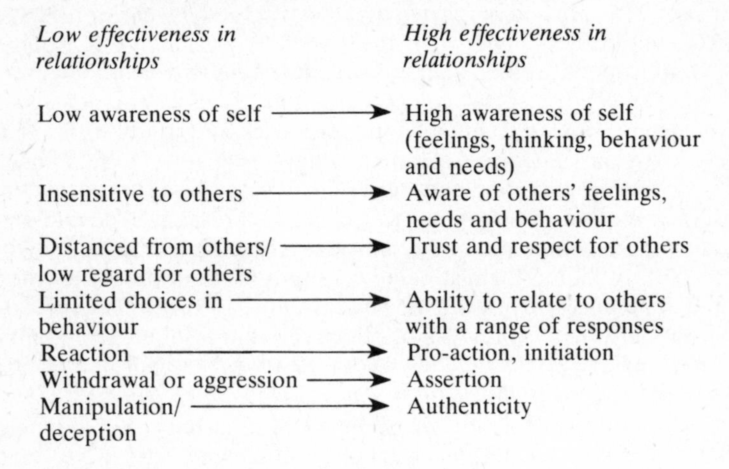

THE AIMS OF TA IN TRAINING TERMS

The question arises: what might these aims look like in training terms? After all, it may not be advisable to state the goals in the language of TA when the meaning of the word has not been elaborated, and there is a risk of people rejecting the approach.

In general terms, TA can be used to aid the following training and development goals in organisations:

1 To improve relationships between people, so that there is less misunderstanding and fruitless 'fighting', and better communication

2 To decrease manipulation, put downs, 'executive politics', and increase straight open honest authentic interaction

3 To increase understanding about 'what goes on' between people

4 To help people grow, develop and increase their sense of self-confidence and self-responsibility

5 To reduce self-defeating behaviours

6 To increase people's ability to assert, i.e. state their wants in a

direct way and get their needs met, as opposed to being aggressive and hostile, devious and manipulative, or withdrawing and avoiding.

These aims overlap considerably and TA is not the only vehicle that is useful in achieving them. They are also not specific in terms of terminal behaviour, partly because the technology is still developing (with increased knowledge and experience it may be possible to become more specific) and partly because this is not in the nature of TA (see Chapter 10). Indeed, improving communications between people and personal growth seems more like a road which we will always be travelling than a destination.

More specifically TA can be used for the following training aims:

1 *To improve particular two-person skills*, e.g. selling, customer contact, consulting and advising, interviewing, appraisal and counselling
2 *To improve group skills*, e.g. leadership and membership skills and the effectiveness of relationships in a team
3 *To develop personal awareness*, e.g. resolving personal difficulties with others, problems of self-image, and the use of passivity or hostility instead of assertion.

The use of TA for these three aims is elaborated by some examples in the following chapters.

THE APPLICATION OF TA

Figure 11.3 gives in summary form the kind of TA input that can be made, in order of increasing personal exposure and commitment (a) to (e), in relation to the overall learning aim and situation. It is by no means a definitive table, but rather a guideline for consideration. For example, developing counselling skills may well involve not only understanding theory, but also skill development (c) and self-awareness development (d) and (e). Exactly what intervention is made will depend on the agreed need and aims, and also on the culture and support of the organisation. For example, personal growth workshops are not advisable where the participants have little or no choice about attending.

GUIDELINES FOR THE APPLICATION OF TA IN TRAINING

This section reviews some important considerations and guidelines in the application of TA. As experience in its use develops, no doubt

Figure 11.3 TA input in relation to the training situation

TA input	*Situation*
(a) *Theory input over limited time*	
Even with its high face validity and ability to catch people's attention, there's a limit to how much 'lecturing' can be done with TA	Presentation to interested parties and key personnel, prior to any training As a component of a wider programme on human relations and man management
(b) *Theory and 'there and then' exercises*	Understanding communications between people, horizontally and vertically
Exercises which deal with a 'generalised person' rather than me and you, e.g. 'describe the style of decision-making used by a manager in each of the four life positions'	
(c) *Theory and ongoing skill practice* TA is used here as an observation tool together with role play practice of the skill concerned, perhaps with CCTV as an aid	Developing selling, customer contact, consulting and advising, interviewing, appraisal and counselling skills
(d) *Theory, and 'here-and-now' exercises* Use of TA to focus awareness and develop interpersonal skills in the 'here and now' (using structured exercises)	Team building. Increasing interpersonal effectiveness. Personal growth, development and problem-solving

(e) *TA as an intervention tool in process groups* The group meet to learn about self and others by studying their own behaviour as it occurs during the life of the group. TA is used to comment on this behaviour, increase personal awareness and help solve problems	Personal growth, development and problem-solving Developing professionals

these guidelines will be modified and extended. In any event in most cases they will remain guidelines rather than become universal laws.

VOLUNTARY VERSUS OBLIGATORY ATTENDANCE AT COURSES

Most managers attend courses without having chosen the course themselves. Many attend on the basis of being sent, willingly or unwillingly, by their organisation, whether because of a specific personal need (e.g. as diagnosed in performance appraisal) or as part of a general career and management development programme run by the organisation. This 'sending on courses' is part of the mutual expectations between employer and employee, whether formal or informal. Some managers are sent decidedly against their wishes and resent this. (How they come to agree to do things they don't want to may be a useful learning opportunity for them in its own right, and one in which TA has a contribution to make.) This general lack of free choice demands careful consideration by the trainer of what is and is not possible. More specifically, unless there is a clear agreement to do so beforehand (as embodied in the course programme, any pre-course notes and a 'contract' with all parties concerned) or a course group decides to move into it, trainers are advised not to use 'here-and-now' exercises and interventions; and even in 'here-and-now' based work, trainers have to be clear about the boundary between training and therapy.

LANGUAGE OF TA

Trainers need to stress with participants that sharing the concepts with the interested and receptive is fine, but imposing them on others with missionary zeal may lead to rejection. Worse still, labelling the uninitiated with the concepts (e.g. 'The trouble with you is that you're a

NIGYSOBer') may lead to bad feelings, outright hostility and resistance to the introduction of TA into that organisation.

BEHAVIOUR OF THE TRAINER

There are some important considerations concerning the behaviour of trainers. Trainers are most effective when confident, i.e. 'OK'. This 'OK-ness' is picked up by the Little Professor and Adult in participants and helps develop a sense of credibility towards the learning and trust in the situation. It is best then for trainers to stay within their limits of confidence, keeping some 'in reserve' as it were, and progressively (through experience and their own training) extend the limits of their abilities. Certainly, since TA is very much about self-responsibility and personal power, if a trainer is feeling low in power through lack of confidence, groups will spot the dissonance between theory in principle (what the trainer is saying) and theory in practice (what the trainer is actually doing). This can all too easily lead to loss of credibility.

Some interpersonal skills trainers have a preference for rescuer behaviour, in common with other members of helping professions (therapists, teachers, social workers, doctors and nurses). The universal risk for rescuers is overwork, exhaustion and insufficient care of self, with a switch to persecutor or victim behaviour. This may be accompanied by loss of energy and enthusiasm, and a reduction in effectiveness.[2] A trainer has to convey not only confidence and power, but also energy, enthusiasm and a sense of well being. This demand for confidence, power, energy and enthusiasm in turn requires that trainers pay attention to themselves in various ways, for example:

1 Ongoing training and development (e.g. courses, reading, reviewing experience)
2 Development of self-knowledge and awareness through peer feedback and workshops. This is extremely important if a trainer is going to help others gain self-knowledge and develop greater effectiveness in relationships
3 Maintenance of health and fitness through relaxation and exercise. Such approaches as meditation can be very helpful in giving a sense of detachment (not 'unattachment') from constant, close involvement with people.

THE ROLE OF THE TRAINER

One important question that all interpersonal skills trainers have to answer for themselves is do they train for 'social adjustment', i.e.

develop managers and staff to perform the tasks and roles currently diagnosed and allocated by the organisation, according to the values and practices of the organisation, or 'social change', i.e. develop organisations, managers and staff in new directions of skill and practice with new choices in behaviour and new ways of performing roles based on new values, with personal growth and awareness as a means of exploring these values and developing the skills involved.

This issue of training for management development or organisation development is one frequently faced by trainers.[3] Certainly some of the assumptions and values of TA listed earlier in this chapter are radically different from those found in many organisations. The trainer who involves himself in work with TA implicitly involves himself in social change, to a degree dependent on the kind of work involved (see Figure 11.3).

CONTRACT

In working with TA, or any form of interpersonal skills training, a trainer is faced with a 'three-cornered contract' situation.[4] This means a situation involving the relationships between himself or herself, the trainee and the organisation who sponsors the trainee as shown in Figure 11.4. This relationship is often simpler in the therapy situation, involving just the therapist and the client, paying for himself or herself. A trainer has to be aware of and influence the three contracts or sets or relationships, and structure his training and intervention according to the agreement reached with the organisation and the participant, and the constraints presented. He may decide that the constraints around will prevent any effective training and it would be better and easier not to undertake the work. Some contra-indications to carrying out effective TA-based training are shown in Figure 11.5. If these are present to any sizeable extent, they would militate against using TA (with the possible exception of making a presentation with further work in mind).

Returning to Figure 11.4, each of the 'contract' areas will be considered in turn. In general terms, the deeper the intervention in terms of Figure 11.3, the more important it is for the trainer to recognise, explore and review the areas with the parties concerned.

The first area is the relationship between trainee and employing organisation. This has some general aspects relating to the overall relationship between the two, as formally recorded and operated in the contract of employment, the job description, the employee handbook and the organisation's formal systems (particularly those originating from the personnel department).

There are also those aspects of an organisation's culture that have to

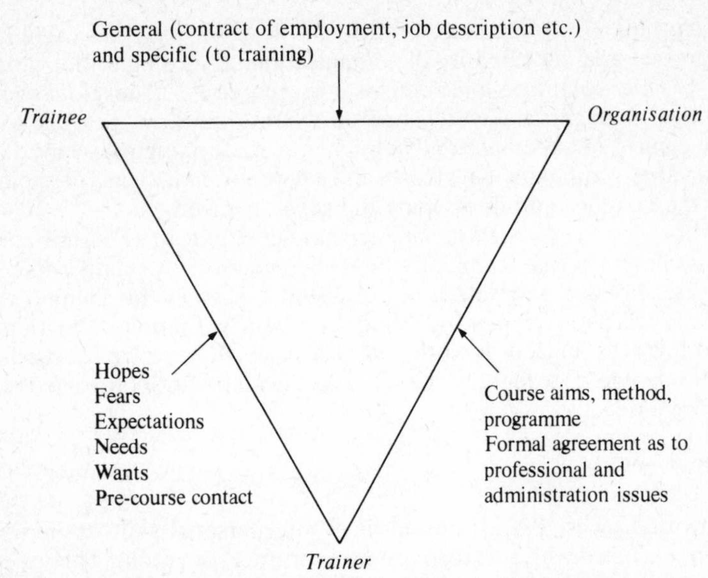

Figure 11.4 Key contracts and relationships in TA-based training – 1

be learnt by new employees. In some cases these may be very important, e.g. does this organisation have autocratic 'theory X' expectations of its employees (which may make the application of TA-based learning difficult) or supportive 'theory Y' expectations (which will make the application of TA easier)? Aspects specific to the role of training in the organisation may also have to be considered, for example:

1 What is the status of training in the organisation?
2 Is it used for punishment, remedial means, reward, personal and career development?
3 Whose responsibility is the training perceived to be (individual, individual's manager, training department)?
4 Who decides the need for training and how?
5 Who chooses the training?
6 To what extent is it obligatory (can an individual say no without detriment to him/herself)?

The second area is the relationship between trainee and trainer. Of course, this is a contract under constant review throughout a course, either explicitly or implicitly. The more explicit it is, the more effective the learning is likely to be and consequently exercises such as 'hopes, fears and expectations' (see Chapter 14) and others aimed at determining needs and wants are useful activities at the beginning of a course. Where the intervention is deeper (e.g. team building or personal

Figure 11.5 Contra-indications to using TA

Participants leaving for home each evening
Training carried out on client's premises, particular work site (with risks of interruptions and with the organisational 'Parent ego state' close at hand)
Team relationships present in learning group, when there is no agreement to focus on these
Training for a specific skill area, when there is no previous experience of this area for trainees to relate to
Insufficient time allowed in relation to aims (in most situations, two days minimum required)
Attention of group elsewhere (e.g. due to work pressure)
Trainer not feeling OK (see p. 98)
Uncertain support from organisation
Unclear agreements with organisation about nature and aims of training
Trainees 'obliged' to be there

awareness courses), pre-course contact such as interviews between trainer and trainees may be important.

As far as the third area is concerned (the relationship between trainer and organisation), a whole range of issues may have to be examined if a deep intervention is being made into personal awareness and team relationships in organisations, and even if the aim is simply development of a particular skill, such as selling or advising. A detailed and explicit statement of training goals, methods and programme may suffice, but the use of a specific record of all professional and administrative aspects as shown in Figure 11.6 is often more sound. The actual content of the record will vary according to whether the trainer is 'internal' (i.e. employed by the organisation) or 'external'.

The three-sided nature of the situation may be complicated in a number of ways. For example, in the case of an external consultant/trainer, there is the extra dimension of the relationship with internal training resources, particularly if they also act as co-trainers. The organisational client may not be one single reference point, but subdivided, e.g. into the managers of the trainees and the top management group, with different wants and expectations about training. Internal trainers are also employees and thus operate in a dual role, mainly as in-house professionals, sometimes as trainees themselves. This may lead to some conflict. For example, when in-company trainers embark on self-development programmes with a personal growth and/or organisational development orientation, not seen as relevant by the organisation, responses of scare and hostility may be triggered.

Figure 11.6 Administrative and professional aspects of trainer–organisation relationship

Professional aspects

(*a*) *Pre-course*

Establish need
Gather data, via interviews and meetings
Decide method(s) of evaluation

(*b*) *Course*

Decide course aims and desired outcomes
Determine methods and technology to be used (see Figure 11.3)
Establish programme of activities for course
Clarify and establish possible and probable consequences, for participants and for the organisation

(*c*) *Post-course*

Agree post-course support and follow-up
Carry out evaluation

Administrative aspects

Establish costs, location, time involved, dates, numbers and names of staff and participants involved, and resources required (rooms, learning and audio-visual aids, etc.)

Consequently, the relationships may be five-sided rather than three, as shown in Figure 11.7. Returning to Figure 11.4, we see a triangle (reminiscent of the drama triangle in Chapter 7) and there is every opportunity in this mesh of relationships to be drawn onto the triangle. For example, a trainer (internal or external) may be invited into a situation:

1 With a view to rescuing someone ('We have a problem and we want you to solve it for us')
2 With a view to persecuting someone ('They're no good and we want you to sort them out')
3 With a view to being persecuted ('Let's get the trainers in. If they don't solve it, we can always dump our bad feelings on them').

In order to avoid being drawn onto the drama triangle, a trainer has to establish the nature of any covert messages and confront them as necessary.

GETTING TA IN – GIVING A PRESENTATION

Sooner or later a trainer may well be given or be able to initiate an opportunity for presenting TA to interested and/or influential people. Such a presentation could usefully cover the key aspects of ego states, strokes, transactions, life positions and games. The following guidelines may be helpful:

1 A balance has to be maintained between running a 'learning' situation and a 'selling' situation. Sufficient opportunity for learning has to be given, so that participants can see the relevance and application of TA. Effective selling has to be achieved as a basis for more meaningful and specific work on future occasions

2 As an aid to effective selling, particular emphasis is required on presentation skills, and the use of clear professional audio-visual aids

3 Also as an aid to effective selling to an organisation, it is useful to have among the participants two key staff groups. First, other personnel and training staff and second, representatives of top management. As a good basis for carrying out further work, the support of these two groups is needed, together with their having an overall understanding of TA concepts. Of course, these two staff groups may be introduced to TA at two different presentations

4 As an aid to learning, the basic concepts of TA need to be covered (with the exception of scripts) together with some exercises to bring the subject to life. Caution is advisable in using 'here-and-now' exercises and making 'here-and-now' interventions because of the limited time and potential authority issues. (Confronting the managing director about his preference

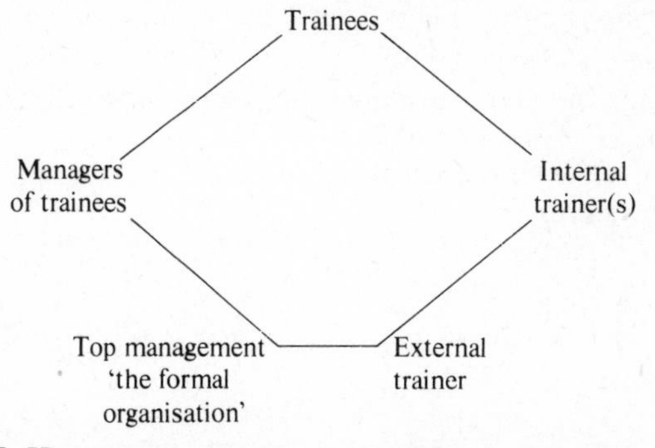

Figure 11.7 Key contracts and relationships in TA-based training–2

for Critical Parent behaviour may not be a wise move in the first half-hour of a presentation!)

5 It is worth spending some time in the presentation looking at the potential areas for use of TA. They include:

selling
customer contact
communication and interpersonal relationships
running meetings
interviewing
coaching
performance appraisal
counselling
influencing
assertion
advising
consulting
time management
management style
group leadership and management
decision-making and problem-solving in groups
participation
team building
organisational change and development
creativity
job enrichment
career development
job performance
personal motivation
personal growth and awareness
women in management
minority groups and race relations at work
safety
induction
conflict management
intergroup relations
negotiating
training trainers

REFERENCES

1 K. Carby and M. Thakur, *Transactional Analysis at Work,* Institute of Personnel Management, 1976.

2 M.D. Mitchell, 'Consultant burnout' in *Annual Handbook for Group Facilitators*, J.E. Jones and J.W. Pfeiffer (eds), University Associates Inc., 1977.

3 J.B. Miner, *The OD – Management Development Conflict*, Business Horizons, December 1973.

4 F. English, 'The Three-cornered contract', *Transactional Analysis Journal*, October 1975.

12 TA and interviewing

TA is, at one level, a theory of communication, and one of the most important uses of communication in organisations is in interviews. On this basis, interviewing is an obvious starting point for the application of TA in organisations.

INTRODUCTION

An interview is any interaction between two people in the context of work. This interaction may be casual, e.g. two colleagues bump into one another in the corridor; or semi-formal, e.g. the same two colleagues after an initial exchange decide to sit down and discuss a particular issue; or formal – planned well in advance and somehow integrated into the personnel systems of the organisation. The list of such planned formal interviews is quite extensive; for example:

recruitment interviews
promotion interviews
appraisal interviews
disciplinary interviews
grievance interviews
welfare and counselling interviews
coaching and target-setting interviews
career development interviews.

All these situations have a common core of activities, i.e. information exchange, problem-solving and decision-making, though the emphasis may be on different activities at different times and some of them may be carried out after the interviews. Two common problems exist with many of these interview situations. First, that the interview and its supporting systems are not accepted by the managers who are responsible for carrying it out. This seems to be a particular problem with performance appraisal, for example, where all too frequently a system is developed by personnel specialists and then imposed on the managers with insufficient consultation. The other problem rife in interviews is that, however sophisticated the supporting systems, the face-to-face situation is frequently managed very badly, and managers are often given insufficient and inadequate training to cope with it.

TA has a positive contribution to make in developing these face-to-face skills. This chapter presents a model for the use of TA in training for interviewing and face-to-face communication skills generally and concludes with a consideration of the application of TA to the recruitment interview. Chapter 12 discusses the use of TA in a very different interviewing situation, that of counselling.

A GENERAL MODEL FOR THE USE OF TA IN TRAINING FOR INTERVIEWING AND FACE-TO-FACE COMMUNICATION SKILLS

THE SETTING

A typical setting for this kind of model would be a course for managers, supervisors and specialists on human relationships and interpersonal skills in organisations. Such a course might be open for all-comers, or designed for one particular organisation. Likely major components to such a course, spread over say five days, would be:

face-to-face communication and interviewing skills
communication in groups, including formal business meetings and informal groups
intergroup communication and negotiation
communication in organisations, including an exercise simulating an organisation.

Clearly, the relationship between the TA-based session and the others would need to be clarified, and some questions answered. For example, do we use TA for looking at communication in groups, or some other model, or both? If we use another model, is it congruent with TA or are there some theoretical or practical contradictions?

THE PARTICIPANTS AND THE NEED

The participants are likely to be twelve to fourteen managers, supervisors and specialists with varying experiences in organisations and varying degrees and kinds of involvement in face-to-face communication, even if they come from one organisation. However, for most people, face-to-face communication is a very significant aspect of their job and this is generally supported by their presence on the course in the first place.

THE AIM

The aim for the course as a whole would be to increase knowledge and skills in interpersonal communication in organisations. Given the nature of the situation and the time available, the aims for the TA-based session are modest. They include:

1 A preliminary introduction to TA
2 Its use in observing and understanding face-to-face behaviour
3 Increased skills in dealing with face-to-face situations.

THE STRUCTURE

The design for this activity over a 1½-day period is shown in Figure 12.1. The three key features – introduction and scene setting, TA input and self-generated role plays – will now be considered in turn.

Figure 12.1 1½-day TA-based programme for interviewing skills

Day 1

9.15	*Introduction and scene setting*	
	Tutor led discussion	What is an interview? What kinds of interviews are there? What goes on between two people in a face-to-face situation? Basic do's and don'ts of interviewing
11.15	*TA: A model for looking at interpersonal behaviour*	
	Theory input	Ego states and exercises Transactions
2.15	*Further TA*	
	Theory input	Strokes and exercises Life positions Games
4.15	*Interview practice: self-generated role plays* Group splits into three subgroups. Subgroups generate interviews based on own experiences, and role plays them on CCTV, using TA as an observation and feedback device	
7.45	*Self-generated role plays: First interview*	

Day 2

9.15	*Self-generated role plays: Second interview*
11.15	*Self-generated role plays: Third interview*

Introduction and scene setting

The aim of this session is:

1 To explore the kinds of two-person situations the participants get involved in in their organisations
2 To relate these to all the possible formal and informal interview situations
3 To elicit from the participants what kind of factors are important to 'me', the other person and the situation, that influence the progress and outcome of an interview
4 To introduce some simple guidelines for managing interview situations more effectively.

The important issue here is that it is better to proceed with the relative sophistication of TA after some of the simple 'dos and don'ts' have been covered.

TA input

Given the short duration of the activity ($1\frac{1}{2}$-days total), only basic theory points are used, as follows: ego states (including contamination and exclusion), transactions, strokes, life positions and games. Games are dealt with quite briefly, focusing on the characteristics of games and the drama triangle as a basic model for looking at games, rather than going into the more elaborate game formula. Some typical games in organisations are quoted, with particular reference to interviewing. Exercises may be used to exemplify the theory, for example the ego-state fantasy exercise (Figure 12.2).

Ego-state fantasies are a useful and versatile method for introducing people to the concept of ego states. Some important aspects in using this approach are:

1 For maximum learning, it is important to ask participants to imagine themselves to be in the situations described, even if they are not typical for them. It may be useful to ask participants to close their eyes as an aid to 'getting inside' the situation
2 As a further help to the learning impact, it is important to build up the situation slowly and carefully, with suitable emphasis on words and phrases
3 At the end of the fantasies, ask the participants to share what they have written down, record on flipchart or overhead and review to 'pull out' examples of ego states

Figure 12.2 Ego-state fantasies

(1)

Imagine you are a boss

You are planning to do a presentation at a meeting, with a subordinate, who is an expert in the field concerned

On the day before the meeting you have a last minute check with him

Some important and powerful people will be present at the meeting

If all goes well, you will gain in status, recognition and responsibility following the meeting

On the day of the meeting, you arrive at 9.20 a.m.

The meeting starts at 9.30. At 9.40, your subordinate has still not arrived, and the chairman decides to begin. The meeting finishes at 11.30, and in the absence of your subordinate, the meeting does not go well for you. At 12.15 you are in your office when your missing subordinate appears

As he walks into your office what are the first few words or phrases you say to him? Write them down

(2)

Imagine you are a subordinate

On Monday your boss asks you to do a report for Wednesday

You say yes, but point out to him that you have a heavy workload

He says that the report must come near the top of your priorities

By Wednesday you have not finished the report because of other demands on your time

You finish the report on Thursday, a full 24-hours late, and take it into his office. As you give him the report, what are the first few words or phrases you say to him? Write them down.

(3)

Imagine you are a member of a section. Your section has just got a new secretary. The previous one had just left after eight years of very good work

This is the second week of having the new secretary. You take her a four-page report for typing

The report is required quickly, and the contents are very important to some senior people

The new secretary duly types the report and returns it to you

There are twenty different typing errors in the report. You return it, pointing out the errors

She retypes the report. On return, there are still ten typing errors. As you return the report for the second time, what are the first few words or phrases, you say to her? Write them down

4 These fantasies can be elaborated and modified or new ones introduced, to increase their relevance to the working situations of the participants.

Self-generated role plays

For this activity, the group is divided into two or three smaller groups, depending on the numbers, and prepares interviews according to the format outlined in Figure 12.3. When developing material for the role playing out of their own experience, participants are given considerable scope to modify and extend. This may be useful for reasons of confidentiality as well as creativity.

The particular advantage in using self-generated role plays is that the material obtained is more likely to be relevant to the organisational situations of the participants than role plays 'imposed' by the trainers. They do take time to 'work up', however.

Each interview is recorded on CCTV, the remainder of the group not involved acting as observers. They are given, say two aspects of the interview to observe as shown on the observation sheet, Figure 12.4.

Figure 12.3 Self-generated role plays

(a) *Individually* think about an incident, real or imagined which might provide the basis of a role play lasting 15–30 minutes (5–10 minutes)

(b) Each person is to describe, briefly, his incident to the other syndicate members (10–15 minutes)

(c) Decide, as a group, which incident you are going to develop into a role play (5 minutes)

(d) Prepare background material ready for briefing the other syndicate. Do not get involved in detailed scripting, but outline the people involved, their jobs and any key factors influencing their behaviour. Decide the role you want a member of the other syndicate to play opposite your own member (15 minutes)

(e) Brief the other syndicate and state which role you want one of its members to play (10–15 minutes)

(f) Listen to the other syndicate's role play briefing. Do not ask questions until the presentation has been completed (10–15 minutes)

(g) Help your role players prepare – strategies, objectives, etc. (15 minutes)

After the close of the interview (each interview normally lasts 25 to 30 minutes), the following review process is used. First, the interviewer and interviewee are asked to share their experiences and conclusions; second, the observers contribute their findings; and third, the trainer adds his own observations and replays on CCTV five or six key aspects of the interview to elaborate points, focus on learning and highlight theory.

Figure 12.4 Observational framework (for observing interviewee, interviewer or both)

Give examples in the interview of:

Behaviour from the Parent ego state
Behaviour from the Adult ego state
Behaviour from the Child ego state
Negative strokes
Positive strokes
Complementary transactions
Crossed transactions
Ulterior transactions

What were the:

Dominant life positions expressed?
Dominant drama triangle positions expressed?

The required style is to avoid declaring rights or wrongs but rather to emphasise choices and consequences, so as not to deflate participants' sense of self-worth. After all, 'performing' on CCTV is a strain for many people and usually means that they start out in their Adapted Child. In any case most participants are probably managing their relationships in organisations reasonably well. The situation is thus viewed as developmental rather than remedial, and the trainees must ultimately decide for themselves if they want to incorporate the new learning and hence add it to their skills. It is interesting that using the self-generated role play method, nearly all the interview situations developed have a high personal problem component, whether appraisal, grievance, disciplinary or counselling in nature. Recurring themes are unsatisfactory job performance, lateness, being passed over for promotion, mistreatment by the manager or organisation and domestic problems giving rise to work problems.

TA AND RECRUITMENT INTERVIEWING

Recruitment interviewing is one of those 'one-sided' situations, like public contact or selling, where the organisational member is 'in the know', while the other party outside the organisation is unlikely to be, thus raising some ethical concerns. Whatever the arguments about this aspect, two things can be said about recruitment interviewing and TA.

SUBJECTIVITY AND OBJECTIVITY IN THE SELECTION PROCESS

The last few decades have seen increasing attempts to make the selection process more systematic and objective through the introduction of personality and vocational testing,[1] systematic interviewing plans[2] and extension of training in interviewing skills. The problem is that, while the systematisation is laudable, there is a limit to how 'objective' and 'scientific' the practice can be made, considering the presence of one vital component, face-to-face human contact. The extension of 'objective' practices frequently implies the exclusion of intuition, a domain not readily amenable to rigorous investigation and control. However, TA suggests that this faculty is very important in human relationships and certainly some selection decisions are, wisely, made on the basis of 'does his face fit', does she/he 'feel right' for the job, as well as all the systematic and objective data. That's the plus side – it may be useful to focus more on intuitive data. On the minus side, the 'feels right for the job' judgement may also mean: 'I, the manager, like to put people down [i.e. an I+ U– life position, or "persecutor"], and this person [according to my "Little Professor"] could make an ideal target [victim].'

APPLICATION

Clearly, an interviewer using TA as a model of behaviour in his head can make judgements about a job applicant's personality and communication style, and relate them to the organisation's requirements in terms of the job and personnel specification. Some of the implications for recruitment interviewing are shown in Figure 12.5. Caution is needed, however. Interviewees in some way 'act' in the recruitment interview situation and this may demand care in interpretation of behaviour. But even in this kind of event TA may help to 'see' beneath the surface of temporary behaviour.

On this basis, TA is a useful choice and resource for advanced recruitment skills training, particularly for personnel professionals, and may be helpful in resolving some specific recruitment problems in organisations. Finally, remember that Berne himself was at one point in his career faced with having to carry out very rapid interviews, for decision-making of a different kind.[3] This led directly to him developing his skills in intuitive assessment and ultimately to the concept of the Little Professor. Many recruitment interviews are also carried out with limited time available, and the conscious development of intuition may well pay dividends here.

Figure 12.5 Some implications of TA for recruitment interviewing

TA concept	*Implications for interviewer behaviour*	*Relationship to interviewee behaviour*
Parent ego states	Pay attention to critical Parent values, attitudes and prejudices in relation to interviewee (e.g. standard of dress). Provide support from Nurturing Parent in potentially stressful situation	Diagnose values and attitudes to job, people, work and organisations
Adult ego state	Clear Adult needed for effective listening skills	Monitor listening, memorising, problem-solving and decision-making
Adapted Child	Interviewer an authority figure	Behaviour may indicate choice of adapted behaviours when faced with authority figures, e.g. compliance, rebellion
Free Child	Source of empathy, curiosity and interest in candidate as a person	Source of motivation
Little Professor	Source of intuitive judgements and perceptions about candidates	Source of creativity
Exclusion	Barrier to interviewer skill (e.g. excluded Adult prevents listening)	Barrier to effective job performance and work relationships
Strokes	Avoid giving negative strokes, give some positive strokes	Interview situation may be seen as negative stroke situation

Life Position	Risk if interviewer moves into I+ U–	Interview situation may be seen in I– U+ terms. Need to move to I+ U+
Trans-actions	Stay mainly in Adult (with NP for rapport building and LP observing) to give mainly complementary transactions	Relative incidence of complementary, crossed and ulterior transactions will give clues to interpersonal and potential managerial style of inter-viewee
Time struc-turing	Stay mainly in activity with support from rituals and pastiming	May be able to diagnose preferred choices of time structuring by interviewee
Games	Barrier to effective interviewing	May be able to diagnose preferred position on drama triangle and hence likely games

REFERENCES

1 F. Sneath, M. Thakur and B. Medjuck, 'Testing people at work', *Information Report* **24**, Institute of Personnel Management, 1976.
2 R. Royde, 'Interviewing techniques' in *Recruitment Handbook*, B. Ungerson (ed), Gower Press, 1975.
3 E. Berne, *Intuition and Ego States*, TA Press, 1977.

13 TA and counselling in organisations

A completely different face-to-face situation from recruitment interviewing is counselling. As a working definition, counselling is helping someone to help themselves resolve here-and-now problems getting in the way of effective work, effective relationships and personal and professional development. It involves the counsellee (or client) changing some aspect of self (attitudes, perceptions, etc.) and the outside world (through behaviour). It *may* involve the counsellor changing some relevant aspect of the counsellee's environment, though only as a support. It is not 'fixing' things for people; it is not just advising people on courses of action; it is not coaching for job performance; and it is not therapy (i.e. changing some substantial part of self and behaviour). It occurs in various settings, e.g. occupational, educational, marital, domestic, religious, etc. In an organisational setting, the counsellor may be a specialist (e.g. from the personnel or training department) or the client's own manager.

COUNSELLING AT WORK

Counselling as an activity is barely recognised by most organisations, and, if it is, frequently has a very low status. There are a few exceptions to this. This general neglect probably relates to the dominant philosphy which regards human resources as a means to an end, such as profitability or power. However, that a need for counselling in organisations exists is clear from several viewpoints:

1 Organisations themselves are important 'stages' for some individuals to act out their script scenes, crises and pay-offs, e.g. getting fired, getting depressed, getting overworked, getting alcoholic, getting power by putting others down, etc.

2 The crises of organisations have severe consequences for the members of that organisation, e.g. losing in the power struggle, becoming redundant in takeovers and financial collapses. Redundancy raises particular problems for men, as so many define their existence by what they do (i.e. work) rather than who they are. Loss of work is all too easily seen as rejection from society. When added to the loss of income involved as well, it is not surprising that redundancy is a very 'not OK' experience for many

3 Change in organisations throws up counselling needs, whether changes in systems and structures or changes brought about by training. This is particularly true when individuals experience human relations and interpersonal skill type training. A minority may well come face-to-face with self-limiting behaviours that require more extensive help. Thus counselling is an almost necessary adjunct to human relations training and an almost necessary skill for the trainers to possess

4 There is an increasing interest in counselling in organisations, as demonstrated by the recent formation of a 'counselling at work' division of the British Association of Counselling (see Appendix 2).

TA AND COUNSELLING

There are many approaches useful to the development of counselling skills each with their own advantages and disadvantages.[1, 2, 3] A particular advantage of TA is its transferability. It is not just a specific model for counselling, but rather a model that can be used to examine and aid all interpersonal situations in organisations, including counselling. Furthermore the language and concepts can be shared with the counsellee giving the opportunity for an educational as well as a counselling relationship. The counsellee can be provided with some conceptual tools to examine his or her own situation and problems. Perhaps most important of all, TA offers ways of dealing with some of the difficulties encountered by counsellors in carrying out their task.

One of the central issues in counselling is: 'Who is responsible for my problem?' Too often the counsellor takes on responsibility for the problem, rescuing the counsellee and acting as a 'Mr Fixit' in providing a solution. This may seem the obvious and quickest route to dealing with people's problems but it can bring disaster in its train. Usually solutions that aren't our own are not carried out too effectively by us. Nor are our skills at managing and solving our own problems developed. Counsellors who rescue this way often find themselves switching to victim on the drama triangle as the counsellee moves to persecutor ('Well, you told me to do so and so . . . but it didn't work. A lot of good your advice was!') as shown in Figure 13.1.

An alternative approach for a counsellor is to put the responsibility for solving the problem fairly and squarely on the shoulders of the

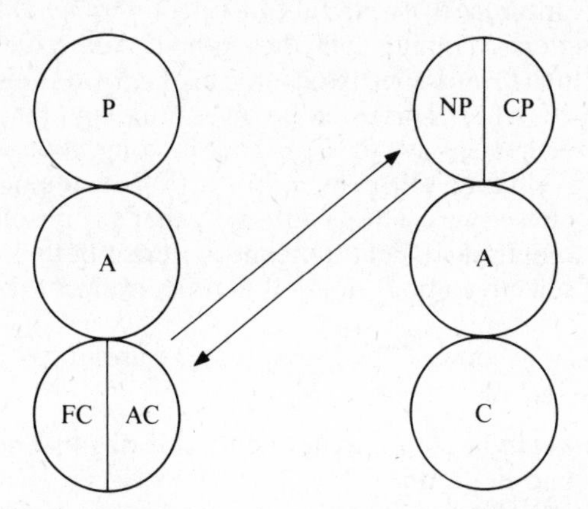

Counsellee: 'I feel so terrible, I just don't know what to do!' [Adapted Child and victim]

Counsellor: 'Never mind, I know it's terrible, I'll tell you what to do....' [Nurturing Parent and rescuer]

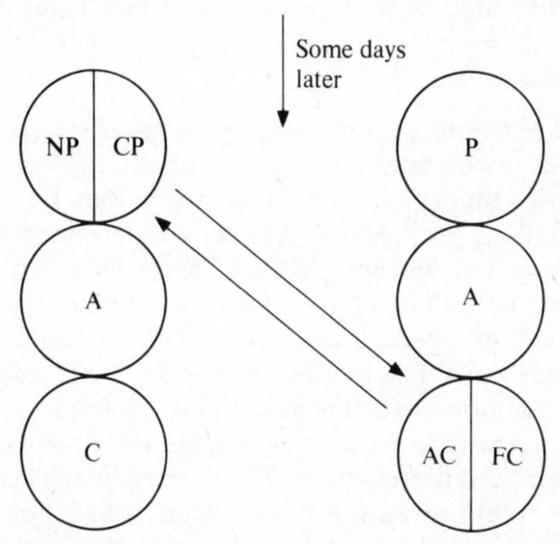

Counsellee: 'Well you told me to do.... but it didn't work. A fat lot of good your advice was!' [Critical Parent and persecutor]

Counsellor: 'Oh .... er ....' [Adapted Child and victim]

Figure 13.1 An unproductive counsellor-counsellee relationship

counsellee (as 'captured' by the definition of counselling at the beginning of this chapter – 'helping someone to help themselves . . .'). In other words, help the counsellee to develop his/her own skills in coping with life and work issues. This often involves building up his/her own sense of self-worth (i.e. I− to I+), and is congruent with TA's emphasis on developing self-responsibility (also a theme of other approaches to counselling). This is not to say that a counsellor should never do or fix something to help someone in a crisis but rather that he or she must be selective about doing it and be aware of the possible consequences.

Some particular aspects of TA theory that are useful to a counsellor in his/her work include:

1 *Contamination* Helping the client to distinguish reality from prejudice and delusion
2 *Exclusion* Helping the client to use areas and resources of thinking, feeling and behaving that he/she has not used before
3 *Games* Helping the client diagnose any games involved in the problems they face. Typical victim games are often at the root of problems that clients bring to counsellors (see Chapter 7). After all, people are unlikely to seek out help unless they feel not OK about themselves.

In the context of training for counselling skills, these concepts need as background an understanding of all the main areas of TA theory, possibly even script theory. A non-winner script may be amenable to change by counselling, but loser scripts may well demand more profound intervention, i.e. therapy. Most of the counsellor's clients in organisations are likely to be non-winners. One further point is that a counsellor can get much data about the dysfunctional behaviours involved in a client's problem by observing what happens in the counsellor's own transactions with the client. For example, the games a client plays with a counsellor may well represent a general problem of behaviour for the client more widely. This is particularly true for those whose problems relate to authority issues, as counsellors are themselves authority figures in their professional capacity. The client–counsellor relationship is then a rich source of data in solving the client's problems.

A COUNSELLING PROGRAMME

A programme for a counselling course with TA as a major component is presented in Figure 13.2, and the important components of the programme are examined below.

A key belief in the programme's operation is that the more self-understanding a counsellor has, the more effective he/she is likely to be in working with clients. It is as important to know what it feels like as a counsellee as it is to possess counselling skills. Various activities are used to help this process of increasing self-understanding, for example:

personal counselling on own problems (counselling practice is after all, central to the programme!)
TA exercises
various group exercises
Gestalt exercises (see page 125).

These activities will be referred to during the description of the programme.

INTRODUCTIONS AND OPENING ACTIVITIES

An example of the activities involved on the first day is shown in Figure 13.3. As the main aim of the programme is to develop skills in a specific two-person situation, these activities have four major themes:

1 To begin the process of 'unfreezing', i.e. getting to know one another and the nature of the learning situation during the week. In TA terms, unfreezing involves reducing Adapted Child behaviours, particularly feelings of fear, anger, confusion and inadequacy, and also responses of rebellion and compliance
2 To begin to define what is meant by counselling and clarify what is involved in counselling
3 To begin to explore what 'we' (the participants) experience in our contact with others in group and two-person situations
4 To help the group develop an identity and integrity of its own. This particular point is very important. If group-level issues such as control, membership, trust and influence are not resolved, they may well interfere in the learning for the week. The development of trust is essential if the participants are to obtain practice in counselling on real-live issues, as opposed to role plays. Hence time is devoted to group-based activities on the first day, even though the aim of the week is related to skill development for a specific two-person situation. Group issues may emerge again later in the week and may need to be resolved before continuing with the main learning, either by direct confrontation between staff and participants and/or by the use of specific structured exercises.

Figure 13.2 A counselling skills programme

Day 1	
1.50 p.m.	Introductions Administration Workshop methods
3.45	Opening activities
7.45	Opening activities continued
Day 2	
9.15 a.m.	Opening activities
10.00	Basic counselling style
10.45	TA theory 1
11.45	Self-generated role plays – preparation
2.15 p.m.	TA theory 2
3.00	Self-generated role plays – preparation
4.00	TA theory 3
4.45	First role play counselling interview
7.45	Second role play counselling interview
Day 3	
9.15 a.m.	TA theory 4
10.45	Third role play counselling interview
2.15 p.m.	Review of counselling interview
4.00	Feedback
7.45	Counselling practice
Day 4	
9.15 a.m.	Counselling practice
10.45	The role of the counsellor and the nature of counselling in organisations
2.15 p.m.	Counselling practice
7.45	Counselling practice
Day 5	
9.15 a.m.	Counselling practice

BASIC COUNSELLING STYLE

In this session, some basic issues of counselling style are presented and discussed, including:

1 The risks of taking responsibility for the client's problem
2 The importance of developing trust before focusing on prob-

Figure 13.3 Opening activities

(1) Paired introductions
Participants interview one another on their work, interests and experience in counselling and then present their partners to the rest of the group

(2) Hopes, fears and expectations

Participants share their hopes, fears and expectations about the course (see Chapter 14)

(3) Group exercise

Participants are instructed as follows:
- (a) Individually list seven qualities of a good counsellor (5 minutes)
- (b) As a group, develop a group list of seven from your individual lists (40 minutes)

At the end of activity, trainers review group's list, add their own comments and then add any comments on group and individual behaviour

(4) 'Impressions' exercise

Participants are instructed as follows:
- (a) In pairs share your first and your current impressions of one another, derived from the day's activities
- (b) Complete this activity with as many of the group as time allows

At the end of activity, trainers review activity, including the process of forming impressions and making contact with some-one new

lem definition and developing steps towards problem resolution. The usefulness of reflecting questions, statements and non-verbals are stressed here (e.g. 'So you're feeling pretty bad, then?', or just head nodding)
3 The risks of judging counsellee behaviour and perceptions and the alternative of helping the client to establish choices and predict consequences
4 The usefulness of checking hunches concerning his or her statements and behaviour with the client directly (e.g. 'It seems to me that . . . Does that fit?')

5 The usefulness of having an interpretative model of human behaviour, namely TA, that can be applied to both the client–counsellor relationship as well as counsellor–third party relationships
6 The use of some basic questions to help define the problem and open up the way to possible solutions (see Figure 13.4).

Figure 13.4 Some basic questions for a counsellor

What is the problem?
Be more specific
How is it a problem?
What are you thinking?
What are you feeling?
What are you doing . . .?
What do you want?
Who is responsible for the problem?
Tell me more about . . .?
What do you expect of me/of yourself in this (counselling) situation?
What are the consequences for you in doing what you are doing?
What are the consequences for others?
How do you stop yourself from changing?
What do you want to change?
How are you going to change?
What are the choices open to you?
What would you say the first step is?
How will it feel if you change?
What are the consequences for you if you change?

A good many of the above have a 'probing' component, and may be asked in a variety of ways. In general the questions are listed in terms of problem definition first and problem resolution second

TA THEORY AND EXERCISES

A fairly extensive input of TA theory is given with emphasis on those aspects of particular use in counselling, as shown in Figures 13.5 and 13.6. Figure 13.5 shows some guidelines for counsellor behaviour based on TA. Figure 13.6 gives a checklist for a counsellor to base observations and interventions on, from a TA viewpoint.

Figure 13.5 Some guidelines for counsellor behaviour

Operate from	Adult (to explore and identify facts, choices and consequences) Nurturing Parent (to take care of your client *and* yourself) Little Professor (use intuition) Free Child (to stay motivated and creative) Occasionally Critical Parent (to prevent someone from being injured) Adapted Child only in extreme cases I+ U+ life position
Be aware of your own	Contaminations Preferred games, rackets and drama triangle position
Avoid	Ulterior transactions Entering drama triangle Stamp collecting
Use	Crossed transactions (where appropriate) Activity and intimacy as major time structuring choices, plus some rituals and pastimes as appropriate

The observations and interventions shown in Figure 13.6 may be related to both the client's here-and-now behaviour and the client's 'problems' with third parties not present in the counselling situation. How the observations are converted into interventions and fed back to the client may vary thus:

1 The observations may be re-interpreted into everyday language, e.g. observation of Parent behaviour – 'You seem to have a rule that . . .'
2 If the client knows TA, the observations may be made directly in TA terms
3 The client may be introduced to TA through the counsellor's interventions, if the situation or time allows, i.e. the relationship becomes an educational one as well as a counselling one.

Exercises are used to help the participants relate the theory directly to their own experiences and behaviour, backed up by small group discussion and feedback, and then reviewed in total group.

Figure 13.6 Observation and interventions checklist with respect to counsellee 'problems' and behaviour, based on TA

Ego states

Dominance of any one?
Facility to behave from all three?
Presence of exclusion?
Nature and extent of contamination?

Strokes

Gives strokes – positive or negative, conditional or unconditional?
Receives strokes – positive or negative, conditional or unconditional?
Accepts or rejects strokes?

Life positions

Dominant life positions?

Transactions

Extent of complementary, crossed and ulterior transactions?

Games

Nature, intensity and pay-offs of games?
Preferred position on drama triangle

Rackets and stamp collecting

Favourite racket(s)?
Extent and type of stamps collected?

Time structuring

Preferred choices

SELF-GENERATED ROLE PLAYS

Rather than use role plays drawn up by the staff, participants are invited to develop their own material relevant to their particular circumstances, as outlined in Chapter 12.

This activity serves to provide an initial structure for the practical work. CCTV is used as an aid, and observers use TA concepts to comment and give feedback on the counselling activity (see Figures 13.5 and 13.6).

PERSONAL COUNSELLING

Any group of average individuals will present a range of issues for potential counselling help. If this is to be capitalised on, sufficient trust in the training situation has to be developed. Working through some self-generated case studies first seems to help in developing this trust. From then on, participants are invited to present their own issues for counselling and to act as counsellors. This may be done in one of two ways, depending on the wishes of the participants involved, either using CCTV, as described in the previous paragraph, or using the 'time-out' approach. In this latter approach, no CCTV is used. The counselling takes place in front of the whole group, with the use of a tape-recorder for recapitulation if required. If the counsellor gets to feel 'stuck', he/she calls for 'time-out' and stops to get advice from first the other participants and then the trainer (who acts as a counsellor to the counsellor – a rather complex situation!) During this process, the client remains silent and may even leave the proceedings.

FEEDBACK

This involves a discussion on giving feedback to clients, including: emphasis on here-and-now behaviour of client; value of contributing comments on counsellor's own thoughts and feelings; and the importance of offering any interpretations, whether TA-based or otherwise, as choices rather than labels.

GESTALT

Gestalt[2, 4, 5] is used as a major support to TA in this course, partly because of its power in emphasising self-responsibility. Gestalt is used in three different ways:

1 Interventions by the staff to focus participants on their own behaviour

2 As exercises to develop self-awareness (e.g. 'Now I am aware . . .', or a fantasy exercise)
3 As the basis for interventions for the participants to make themselves in their counsellor role.

THE ROLE OF THE COUNSELLOR AND THE NATURE OF COUNSELLING IN ORGANISATIONS

During the practical activities, a range of issues and problems are usually raised concerning the role of the counsellor and the nature of counselling in organisations. These are reviewed towards the end of the course, and some of the important ones are discussed in this section. The starting point is the client, who usually:

experiences him or herself as a victim
is stuck in this position in some way
disclaims responsibility for the situation or problem
is invested in the (negative) pay-off to the problem and in getting the negative strokes involved
invites the counsellor to rescue.

This assumes of course, that employees are prepared to present themselves as clients to an in-house counsellor in the first place. There may be two reasons why they don't. First, negative perceptions of counsellors abound (sometimes with a justifiable basis) and stereotypes, e.g. 'spy', 'judge', 'shrink', may well 'block' individuals seeking counselling. The second is that the client–organisation relationship may be unhelpful to effective counselling, through either role expectations ('You're here to work, counselling has nothing to do with employment') or cultural expectations ('We expect men to grin and bear it and get on with the job'). In any case they may be present under duress (e.g. 'sent' by their boss, against their will). This may need direct confrontation by the counsellor even to the extent of declining to work with the intended client.

Assuming that potential clients overcome their negative perceptions and the role and cultural expectations in the organisation do not offer a serious barrier, the next issue is what are the goals of a counsellor in his/her work with a client? Some of the key ones influenced by TA are:

1 Develop a relationship of caring and trust, and ultimately a sense of 'protection',[6] TA concept meaning in essence 'everything will be OK. The problem is resolvable in some way'
2 Establish self as a credible figure, potent, skilful and effective (but not omnipotent)
3 Avoid entering the drama triangle, i.e. offer help but not rescuing

4 Separate myth from reality with the client
5 Confront incongruities and discrepancies in the client's attitudes and behaviour
6 Emphasise personal power and responsibility of the client
7 Help the client to stop taking responsibility for others' feelings and behaviour
8 Help the client define the problem
9 Help the client generate alternative courses of action for resolving problems.

Exactly which of these goals is pursued and how will depend on the 'contract' the counsellor has with the client. The notion of contract, and clarity of contract, is an important one in TA, referred to in Chapter 11. By contract is meant the set of assumptions, expectations, aims and goals that define our relationship and work together. The more explicit the contract is made, the more effective our relationship is likely to be. In counselling, as in training the counsellor is faced with a 'three-cornered' contract situation. The relevance and importance of the client–organisation relationship has already been explained in the form of role and cultural expectations and the voluntary versus obligatory presence of the client for counselling.

As far as the relationship between counsellor and client is concerned, there are four possible basic contacts, which may occur in combination:

1 Agreement by counsellor to 'fix' something for client. This may be necessary in a crisis and when the counsellor determines that other sources of help are needed to deal with the client's problems
2 Agreement by counsellor to help client change from feeling bad to feeling good. This is often an implicit contract and involves the client in discharging stored-up feelings, openly expressing him or herself about an issue, getting something off his/her chest, even openly crying. Here the goal of the counsellor is the first of the list presented earlier, i.e. developing a situation of trust and caring and giving the counsellee 'space' (to reflect)
3 Agreement by counsellor to help client resolve problems through stopping certain behaviour or actions, e.g. stop being late for work. The difficulty here is, if the client has energy invested in doing something ('being late') and then invests energy the opposite way ('stopping being late'), this one issue is soaking up much of the client's personal energy
4 Agreement by counsellor to help client resolve problems through starting new behaviours and actions. This requires the counsellor to work to all the goals listed earlier and getting a

verbal agreement from the client – 'From now on I will . . .'.

The last is often the most satisfactory contract for a counsellor to achieve with a client, from the viewpoint of both parties. Evaluating counselling work poses problems not unlike those of social skills training. However, a hard contract for changing behaviour in some specific way gives the opportunity for checking effectiveness, through arranging follow-up meetings after one or a series of counselling sessions.

One final point on the counsellor–client relationship is that it is inherently stressful, even if the counsellor avoids rescuing (see also for trainers, Chapter 11). This demands that the counsellor manage his/her work load by not taking on too many clients and by planning sessions in a realistic sequence and timing. (This is not easy when presented with 'crises' that won't wait or when working in a personnel or training function, with other responsibilities.) It also demands attention to personal, physical and emotional well-being, as well as ongoing development to maintain confidence and skill.

The third relationship in the three-cornered contract is that between counsellor and organisation. For someone to work in a counselling role effectively, a clear contract is needed with the organisation concerning a number of issues. For example:

1 Formal recognition of counselling as an integral part of, say a manager or specialist's role, through addition to the individual's job specification, is strongly recommended. Counselling on one's own initiative may well lead to being persecuted by the organisation
2 Whether the counselling is to cover just work-related problems, or the more general problems of employees needs to be established
3 Role conflicts may exist with respect to other job demands. For example, the management development adviser who is involved in counselling and also in career and succession planning may well have problems over confidentiality. The manager who wants to counsel, but is also required to judge, may have problems in gaining trust
4 Conflicts between client needs and organisational needs may place a great strain on confidentiality, particularly if there is a legal dimension, e.g. someone has been 'fiddling the till'
5 Recognition by the organisation of external sources of help and the counsellor's role in contacting these sources is necessary
6 The organisation needs reassurance that the counsellor is clear on the boundary between counselling and therapy (for example, not encouraging a counsellee to regress to an earlier age).

In conclusion, the basic three sets of relationships a counsellor is involved in present risks of being drawn into the drama triangle, most usually in the way shown in Figure 13.7. The clearer a counsellor is about his contract with the organisation and his contract with the client, the less likely he or she is to be drawn into the drama triangle, and the more effective the counselling.

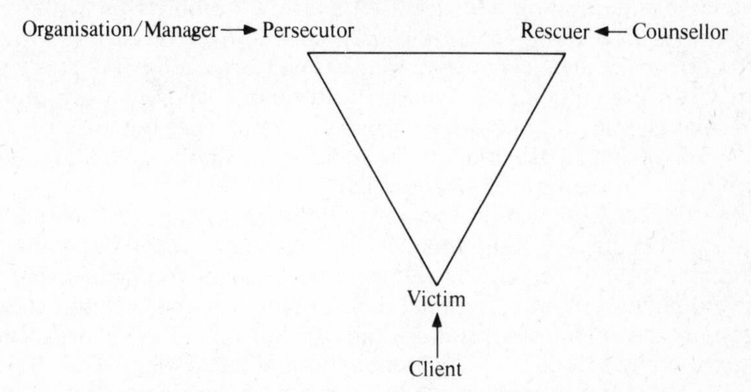

Figure 13.7 Counselling and the drama triangle

REFERENCES

1 R.R. Carkhuff, *Helping and Human Relations*, vols. I and II, Holt, Rinehart and Winston, 1969.
2 W.R. Passons, *Gestalt Approaches in Counselling*, Holt, Rinehart and Winston, 1975.
3 J. Southgate and R. Randall, *The Barefoot Psychoanalyst; An Introduction to Karen Horney Counselling*, Book One, The Association of Karen Horney Psychoanalytic Counsellors, 1976.
4 F. Perls, R.F. Hefferline and P. Goodman, *Gestalt Therapy: Excitement and Growth in the Human Personality*, Dell Publishing Company Inc., 1951.
5 S.H. Herman and M. Korenich, *Authentic Management: A Gestalt Approach to Organisations and their Development*, Addison-Wesley, 1977.
6 C.M. Steiner, *Scripts People Live*, Grove Press Inc., 1974; Bantam Books, 1975.

14 TA and advising

One of the significant phenomena in the development of organisations since the Second World War has been the growth of the specialist. In this context a specialist is someone who has particular expertise to offer the organisation and does not exercise authority by virtue of hierarchical position. He or she may not be involved in the power structure at all, and may be operating as an external adviser or consultant. Such a role demands abilities to influence and get work done through people, not only from a position of expertise but also from a position of interpersonal skill, in some ways similar to selling and public contact skills (see Chapter 18).

Such specialists include not only computer, operational research, industrial engineering and financial experts whose expertise is 'quantitative', but also personnel, training, safety and health, management development and organisational development experts, whose expertise is to do with human resources and relationships in some form. The case of organisational development experts is interesting.[1] The 1950s and 1960s saw the rapid growth of organisation development (OD) as an area of knowledge and as a profession for the application of behavioural sciences to organisational needs. One important development during the growth of this knowledge was to recognise that the quality of the relationship between adviser/consultant on the one hand and client on the other was as important to a successful outcome as the quality of the actual expertise offered. Indeed, the opportunity for change that any expert offers to a client actually starts at the first meeting between expert and client, not at the first application of the expert's technology (whether carrying out an attitude survey, starting a Management by Objectives programme or running a course). Consequently OD experts have paid considerable attention to the dynamics of their relationships with their clients.[2]

TA also offers ways of managing the adviser/consultant–client relationships more effectively. In fact, TA and OD are not exclusive approaches and can be used jointly. As an example of the contribution TA can make in this area, let us look at an example, namely the handling of a client in Critical Parent (Figure 14.1).

There may be times when it is appropriate to apologise in the manner shown in Figure 14.1. Suppose, however, that this is a repetitive situation for these two people, i.e. the client typically relates from Critical Parent and the adviser habitually responds in a stereotyped way from Adapted Child. TA shows that there are some other choices, as in Figures 14.2, 14.3 and 14.4. In other words, we can use TA to help advisers and consultants develop a greater response range in their

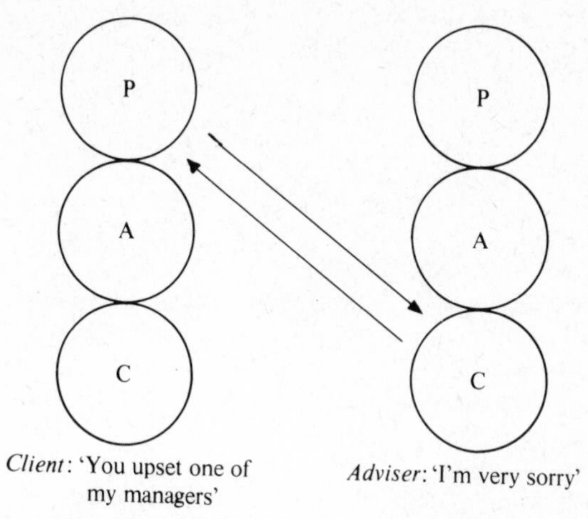

Figure 14.1 Adapted child response from adviser

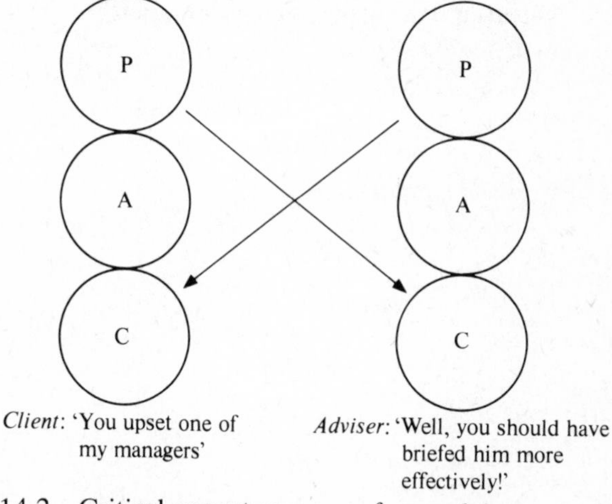

Figure 14.2 Critical parent response from adviser

interpersonal relationships.

The example quoted is typical of situations that advisers and consultants face, particularly if there is an 'inspecting' quality to their roles. A consultant can be seen as someone who is outside the power system of a group who in turn define themselves as needing help and initiate a voluntary and temporary relationship with the consultant to provide that help. This represents the situation of many external consultants, but not internal advisers or those external consultants/advisers with a legislative and inspecting base to their role, e.g. training

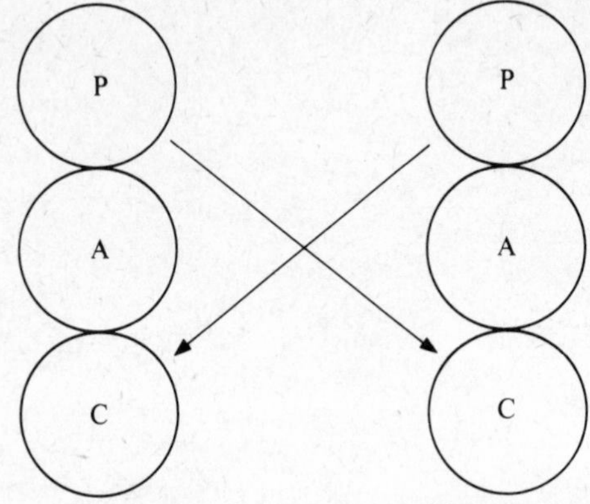

Client: 'You upset one of my managers'

Adviser: 'I know you and your team are under pressure, and things are a bit tough at the moment, I'm sure we can help you sort it out'

Figure 14.3 Nurturing Parent response from adviser

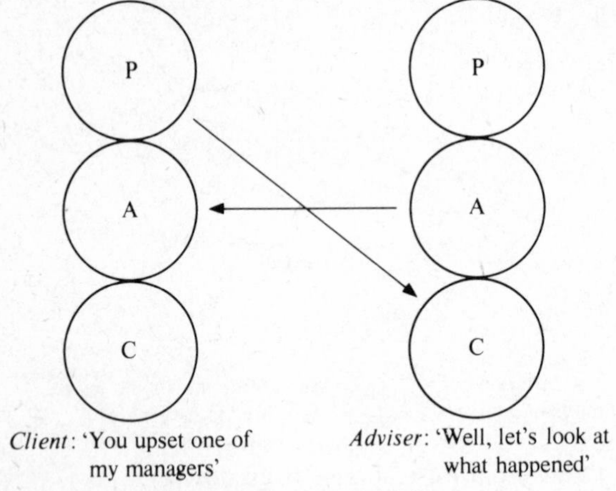

Client: 'You upset one of my managers'

Adviser: 'Well, let's look at what happened'

Figure 14.4 Adult response from adviser

board advisers. In response to this 'inspection' possibility, some clients are likely to react defensively from Critical Parent.

The sections that follow show examples of the use of TA in developing advising skills. The two examples are the training of training board advisers and the training of specialist financial advisers.

In both cases, the work centres on the needs of specific organisational groups, and other training approaches were combined with the TA.

USE OF TRANSACTIONAL ANALYSIS TO DEVELOP ADVISING SKILLS FOR ADVISERS IN THE ENGINEERING INDUSTRY TRAINING BOARD

THE SETTING

The 1960s saw the advent of legislation to promote more effective training in a wide variety of organisational settings. The main instruments for this promotion are the industrial training boards and their staff – the training advisers. Board staff mostly operate as advisers on training needs and standards rather than as face-to-face trainers, except for specialist teams, and spend considerable time working with key figures in client companies. This places great onus on an adviser's skills at an interpersonal level as well as at a technical one. It is with this background in mind that the following course has been designed and mounted for the Engineering Industry Training Board (EITB) over the last few years.

THE NEED

The EITB invests time in its new recruits to develop knowledge of training technology and also of board policies and practices, as would be expected. A need was also perceived to develop skills in effective advising and presenting of board requirements, resources and expertise, and also to manage more effectively the dual nature of the role (i.e. advising and 'inspecting' or monitoring).

PARTICIPANTS

There are between eight and fourteen relatively newly recruited advisers with some limited field experience, on each course.

OBJECTIVES

The aims of the course are to give participants an opportunity:

1 To develop general insight into behaviour in a 1 : 1 situation
2 To develop awareness and skills in handling the relationship between adviser and client
3 To improve the adviser's skill at gaining acceptance by a company and managing his/her relationship with the key personnel involved
4 To improve the adviser's skill in joint problem-solving and the diagnosis of company needs

5 To develop the adviser's ability to influence the company to train in accordance with board approaches
6 To give guidance in relating the above objectives to the 'on-the-job' situation.

THE COURSE

As stated, participation on the course is part of the induction process for the advisers and not voluntary, and this influences the structure of the course (see Chapter 11). In the first instance, brief pre-course notes are sent out to participants in order to begin clarifying expectations about the course and to influence the trainer–trainee relationship. These notes refer to the use of TA on the course. The approach to learning is to use a cycle of short theory inputs, practical activities and review sessions. In the practical sessions there is a strong emphasis on increasing people's choices for behaviour in the advising situation, rather than affirming rights or wrongs. The course is flexible to meet the emerging needs of the group of participants, so that the actual order of events and precise content will vary from one programme to the next. The main inputs to the course are TA theory, activities to illustrate the theory, role playing exercises focusing on client–adviser relationships, and some non-TA based theory that examines the client–adviser relationship.

The course runs over a five-day period, starting on Monday evening. A typical outline programme (also sent to intending participants) is shown in Figure 14.5, but this is only an indication of the probable order of events and is not a rigid timetable. Note that 'Theory – Interpersonal behaviour' refers to TA, and 'Theory – The advising relationship' refers to other non-TA theory. Some of the key features of the programme, including the use of TA, are elaborated in the next section. The content of the programme has changed over the years.

KEY FEATURES OF THE ADVISING SKILLS COURSE FOR EITB ADVISERS

EXCHANGE OF EXPECTATIONS (Monday evening)

After personal introductions, the total group is split into small groups of three or four to examine and report back on the following three questions:

1 'What are your wildest hopes for the week?'
2 'What are your worst fears for the week?'
3 'What are your reasonable expectations for the week?'

Figure 14.5 Outline programme for advising skills course

Monday

6.30 p.m. Arrival
Introductions
Exchange of expectations
Workshop methods and objectives

Tuesday

Theory – interpersonal behaviour (1)
First exercise and analysis
Theory – interpersonal behaviour (2)
Second exercise and analysis
Theory – interpersonal behaviour (3)
Preparation for third exercise – self-generated role plays
Third exercise – interviews and analysis

Wednesday

Theory – interpersonal behaviour (4)
Third exercise – interviews and analysis continued
Theory – interpersonal behaviour (5)
Preparation for the fourth exercise – 'training officer' role play
Fourth exercise – interviews and analysis
Fourth exercise – interim analysis
Theory – the advising relationship (1)

Thursday

Theory – the advising relationship (2)
Fourth exercise – further interviews
Fourth exercise – final analysis
Theory – the advising relationship (3)

Friday

'Back home' planning
Feedback to trainers

Each small group usually gathers three or four items under each question and their responses are posted on flipcharts on the walls, so that they are available for immediate discussion and for ongoing review during the week. This fairly standard approach to starting experiential learning workshops serves the important purpose of establishing the trainer–trainee 'contract' (Chapter 11) and of clarifying mutual expectations over such issues as:

confidentiality
balance of theory and practice
nature of the feedback given during practical activities
use of jargon
the extent to which the situation is therapeutic or educational
who is responsible for the learning
what will be the behaviour of the trainers
the divergent nature of the learning
the flexibility of the programme.

Some typical comments are shown in Figure 14.6. Note that the staff also do a 'hopes, fears and expectations' sheet.

THEORY – INTERPERSONAL BEHAVIOUR (Tuesday and Wednesday)

Transactional analysis is used as the major theoretical input in the course, normally in the following sequence:

Ego-state fantasies

Three 'scenes' taken from organisational contexts are described to participants who are asked to give their personal responses, as in Chapter 12.

Figure 14.6 Some typical 'hopes, fears and expectations' comments

(Wildest) hopes

'Greatest course ever'
'Will be able to deal with every conceivable client after the course'

(Worst) fears

'Course will be a failure'
'The theory will be boring'

(Reasonable) expectations

'I shall get something valuable and usable this week'
'I shall have some new ways to deal with some of my difficult clients'

Ego-state theory

At this point, the functional aspects of ego states are presented, together with the ideas of contamination and exclusion. Ongoing reference is made to organisational situations and client behaviour, and also to the group-generated words and phrases recorded from the ego-state fantasies.

Ego-state questionnaire

To gain greater understanding of ego states, some questions modified from Jongeward and James' ego-state reaction quiz[3] are given to participants in small groups, see Figure 14.7. The small groups present their responses to the total group and the discussion that follows gives an opportunity to expand understanding.

Strokes

The concept of strokes is presented, and to get a greater awareness of the idea, participants are asked to consider how they typically give and receive positive and negative strokes.

Life positions and transactions

These concepts are presented next. To give a greater understanding of the idea of transactions, two cameos of typical scenes from the adviser–client relationship are presented to the group. An example is shown in Figure 14.8.

Working in trios (one as the 'training adviser', one as the 'training manager', one as 'observer') the training adviser 'says' first from Parent ego state whatever seems appropriate for the situation. The training manager responds to this transaction and the observer diagrams the initial transaction, the response and whatever transactions follow. The exercise is repeated with the training adviser in Adult, and then again in Child ego state. The trio share their observations and experiences, focusing particularly on how it felt to behave in different ego states and what the consequences of each initial transaction were.

After one cycle of initiation and responses from different ego states, the roles of 'adviser', 'manager' and 'observer' are switched round. This gives people a very full opportunity to experience themselves in different ego states and transactions and also experience in observing others, using TA as a model.

Figure 14.7 Ego-state questionnaire

Identify each reaction to the situation as Critical Parent, Nurturing Parent, Adult, Adapted Child or Free Child

1 A junior clerk loses an important letter

(a) 'Why can't you keep track of anything you're responsible for?'
(b) 'Check each person who may have used it in the last two days and try to trace it. Perhaps Mrs Smith can help you.'
(c) 'I can't solve your problems. I didn't take your old letter.'

2 A piece of equipment breaks down

(a) 'See if a repair man can come this morning.'
(b) 'Damn! This machine is always breaking down. I'd like to throw it on the floor and jump on it!'
(c) 'Those operators are so careless! They should know better!'

3 The boss is not satisfied with a letter his secretary wrote in reply to a memo from another department. She replies:

(a) 'Good heavens, Mr Smith, I read that memo three times and it's so bad I just can't figure it out. He must be an idiot!'
(b) 'I found the memo contradictory, Mr Smith. I'd find it quite helpful to hear what you think is his main question.'
(c) 'We shouldn't have to answer this memo at all. That man clearly doesn't know what he's talking about!'

4 Tea break gossip reports a colleague is about to be transferred

(a) 'Boy, tell me more. I'd like to get something on George. He gives me a pain in the neck!'
(b) 'Let's not spread a story that may not be true. If we have a question, let's ask the boss.'
(c) 'We really shouldn't talk about poor old George. He has so many troubles – financial, marital, you name it.'

Figure 14.8 Transactional cameo

> In your role as training adviser, you have made an appointment to see the training manager at a client firm, at his request. When you arrive, you are told by his secretary that he is away at a meeting. He finally arrives back from the meeting one hour late. You say . . .

Other TA theory

Other TA theory, including games and the drama triangle, stamps and time structuring, is presented in the context of the practical activities described in the next two sections, i.e. the theory is 'pulled-out' in response to the practical events. Of all the concepts, the drama triangle is one of the most vivid for describing some of the relationships issues facing training board advisers. Many clients see themselves as 'victims' of the boards and attempt to handle this by switching and 'persecuting' the advisers.

SELF-GENERATED ROLE PLAYS (Tuesday and Wednesday)

For this activity participants are subdivided into three small groups and asked to develop role plays based on their own experience or concerns as training advisers according to the directions show in Figure 12.3. Using a member of another small group as adviser, the role plays are re-enacted on CCTV, with all the other participants observing. Each observer is briefed to look at two or three of the dimensions listed in Figure 12.4. Each of three interviews in total is reviewed by participants, observers and staff, with particular emphasis on feedback for the participant in the adviser role.

TRAINING OFFICER ROLE PLAY (Wednesday and Thursday)

This is based on a case study concerning an organisation with a number of training problems. A member of staff plays the role of education and training manager, and the participants divide into three teams of advisers. Each team has an interview with the client involving one or two of their members. The interview is recorded on CCTV with non-interviewing team members observing during the recording. Each advising team is then given the tape of the recording to review for themselves, with two goals in mind:

1 To plan their tactics for a second interview
2 To select highlights for presentation to the total group for

further discussion and feedback, using the concepts developed during the week.

After the first round of interviews with each of the three teams, the highlights are reviewed in the total group, and a second round of interviews run. This is succeeded by a further opportunity for review in each advising team, followed by presentation to the total group.

Using this exercise and the one in the previous section, most participants will have had an opportunity to experiment with and get feedback on their behaviour as advisers in a supportive and constructive environment.

THEORY – THE ADVISING RELATIONSHIP (Thursday)

Short inputs are made on non-TA theory to gain some other perspectives on the adviser's role and relationships.

Organisation development theory

Some inputs are given from organisation development thinking,[1,2] such as the range of styles open to the adviser.

The adviser's power base

A discussion group is held on the sources of power for the adviser, whether legislative, structural or personal.

The adviser as a representative

This involves a discussion on the relationship between the adviser and the board. The experiences of those participants watching their colleagues interviewing the 'education and training manager' is a useful practical starting base for this. As they are watching their colleagues, they may think of all kinds of things for him or her to say, or not to say. However, they are not able to intervene in the 'here-and-now' of the interview, which in some ways parallels the relationship between the 'centre' of an organisation and its representatives in the field.

BACK HOME PLANNING (Friday morning)

Finally, time is devoted to give the participants practice in counselling. Many advisers and consultants experience their clients from time to time asking for help that is more to do with personal counselling than technical consulting (see Chapter 13). It seems important that they have some skills in this sphere for use where the personal issue is preventing effective work at a technical level. The participants are given an opportunity to practise these skills in the following way. The group is divided into small groups. One person operates as counsellor, one as counsellee and the rest as observers. The counsellor then helps the counsellee, using TA as an aid, with an issue facing the latter when he or she leaves the course, particularly an issue to do with applying what has been learned to his/her own client relationships and skills as an adviser.

In briefing the group for this activity typical guidelines given include staying clear of certain games, e.g. 'Why don't you . . ., Yes, but . . .', and generally avoiding the rescuer and persecutor positions in the drama triangle. The observers give feedback to the counsellor on his/her style and choices and then the roles are moved around the group.

USE OF TA TO DEVELOP ADVISING SKILLS IN A FINANCIAL SETTING

THE SETTING

The setting for this work was in a division of a major financial institution. The division concerned was responsible for developing a range of computerised services for a wide customer mix in a near monopoly situation. The division was organised on a project/team basis and the structure was constantly being altered to take into account the changing priorities of the systems being developed. One group had the responsibility for liaising between the internal computer design and operational teams on the one hand and clients on the other. This liaison group consisted of seven section heads (four of whom reported directly and three indirectly to the group manager) and twenty-one advising staff responsible to the section heads, many of them newly recruited.

THE NEED

The situation that the group faced was that the changing computer systems of the organisation meant changes in the services offered to the clients, and it was the liaison group's responsibility to:

> Keep the clients up to date with the proposed changes; and
> help the clients manage the impact of the changes.

The section heads of the liaison group and the internal training department had reached agreement that training might be able to help the group to carry out its job more effectively. However, the best way of dealing with this training need was not at first clear, and various approaches had been considered.

This uncertainty highlights the requirement for pre-course investigation of the learning needs before running a TA course for a specific group (or running any kind of training course). As a consequence two meetings were held with section heads to clarify the needs. The main external problem areas identified were:

hostility and aggression by clients
resistance to change from clients
interpersonal skills of advisers
changed allegiance of some of the advisers who had been recruited from the client organisations
requirement for flexibility of behaviour in advisers
past agreements to the clients about the services offered were sometimes not met
some overlapping of responsibilities among advisers due to the organisation of the various teams
differences in the power clients could use to influence the changes in technology and services offered (by the financial organisation)
variation in size of client organisations from 20+ up to 1,000+ people
clients at different levels of change in relation to the changing technology
informal intercommunication between client organisations sometimes leading to problems for the advisers
the basic problem of the constantly changing technology and organisational structure.

Some of these problems are structural and technical, some interpersonal and some a mixture.

In addition, there were internal problems relating to relationships within sections of the liaison group. Whilst the problems presented would have been amenable to a wider organisational development programme it was decided, because of limitations of time and money, to tackle the interpersonal relationships area. During the discussions with the section heads, the felt needs crystallised into:

selling, 'unselling', 'reselling' skills
advising and client-motivating skills
skills in handling conflict and hostility.

This in turn gave a general training aim of improving the interpersonal skills of members of the liaison group with particular reference to their role as advisers to clients, through increasing their understanding of the options available to them and increasing their ability to make more effective choices of appropriate styles in a range of situations.

In summary, the first steps in the overall programme were:

1 Meetings with the section heads leading to the identification of problems
2 The isolation of some learning needs
3 The establishment of an overall training aim.

The culture of the group was one of 'doing' rather than thinking, and goal-orientated rather than procedure-orientated, which suggested a highly participative course would be most suitable. In addition, the advising role, with a preponderance of 1:1 situations, suggested TA as a suitable major input. This was endorsed by the 'temporary' nature of the group (the ongoing technical changes would almost certainly mean structural changes in the near future, and in any case many of the members were on short-term contracts). TA is very appropriate to this situation as it appears to be more easily retained by individuals after a course than some other group-dependent approaches to interpersonal skills training.

The next step was a meeting between the external consultant and the two members of the organisation's training department to clarify goals and establish the technology and design of the course. Because of the numbers involved, two courses were agreed, of 2½-days' duration, run within a fortnight of one another.

PARTICIPANTS

There were fourteen or fifteen members and section heads of the liaison group per course and two courses in total.

GOALS

These were stated as follows:

1 To increase the understanding and awareness of the range of skills available to participants in the liaising and advising role
2 To help them make more soundly-based choices on the appropriate style and tactics for a range of advising situations
3 To give participants some understanding of people's reaction to change and help them to be better equipped to develop trust, commitment and motivation with clients.

THE COURSE

Each course was run over a three-day period in a non-residential setting. Many aspects of the courses were similar to the training board advising skills courses already described.

1 Brief pre-course notes were sent out to participants in order to clarify expectations about the courses. These notes stressed that a particular approach would be used for looking at advising skills and interpersonal relationships, and that participants would not be in any way put at risk. 'Transactional analysis' was not mentioned
2 The approach to learning during the course was composed of a cycle of short theory inputs, practical activities and review sessions
3 TA was used as the main model for looking at behaviour
4 The experience of the participants themselves was used as a major component
5 Emphasis was placed on increasing people's choices in the advising situation rather than affirming rights or wrongs in behaviour
6 Whatever the course design agreed, flexibility of choice was kept to meet the emerging needs of the participants. Indeed, the second programme did differ from the first as a result of the trainers' experiences.

Some significant differences from the training board advising skills courses were:

1 Because of the short time period of the course and the relatively large size of the groups, the use of CCTV was ruled out
2 The staff team was made up of two internal trainers acting in ancillary roles to the external consultant (see p. 150)
3 Both the pre-course notes and the programme excluded any mention of TA. This decision was based on the evidence that the publication of *any* 'behavioural jargon' beforehand would increase resistance to learning amongst some participants, making their involvement in the programme more difficult (see Chapter 11)
4 As an aid to dealing with excessive Critical Parent behaviour in clients, the use of assertion skills techniques was introduced
5 The courses related to a 'one-off' need, rather than an ongoing induction situation.

KEY FEATURES OF THE ADVISING SKILLS COURSE FOR LIAISON GROUP ADVISERS

The outline programme for each course is as shown in Figure 14.9, and the various activities detailed below.

INTRODUCTIONS

As discussed in Chapter 11, it is important to clarify the nature of the training experience as much as possible with participants before get-

Figure 14.9 Outline programme for the advising skills courses for the liaison group

Day 1

Start – 12.00 a.m.
Introductions
Small group discussion – 'Issues I face with my clients'
Lunch – 1.00 p.m.
Theory and exercises – personality and attitudes of clients and their reactions to change
Small group discussion – 'The types of client I deal with'
Finish – 5.30 p.m. approximately

Day 2

Start – 9.45 a.m.
Review of previous day's work
Theory and exercise – relationships with clients
Lunch – 1.00 p.m.
Discussion – dealing with difficult clients
Theory and small group discussion – understanding hidden messages and manipulation by clients
Finish – 5.30 p.m. approximately

Day 3

Start – 9.45 a.m.
Review of previous day's work
Discussion – dealing with difficult clients (continued)
Theory and small group discussion – expanding range of skills for use in advising situations – developing commitment
Lunch – 1.00 p.m.
Small group discussion – new ways of dealing with clients
Course review
Finish – 4.00 p.m. approximately

ting into the real substance of a course. Time did not allow a full 'hopes, fears and expectations' activity as in the training board advising skills workshops, and consequently the staff presented their view of the course using the pre-course notes as a basis. An opportunity was given for the participants to question the trainer's view of the course and contribute theirs.

'ISSUES I FACE WITH MY CLIENTS'

The session had three phases, an individual, a small group and a total group phase, as outlined in Figure 14.10. The session had two aims:

1 To familiarise participants with the learning approach
2 To begin focusing people on relationships problems as a basis for further work. During the total review, after the small group work, the problems listed were split into organisational and relationships-orientated ones. This was to separate out the organisational and structural ones, largely outside the influence of the participants, so as to help focus on those more to do with interpersonal behaviour.

Figure 14.10 'Issues I face with my clients'

1. Individually, focus on the difficulties and problems (but not technical ones) you face with clients, particularly in relation to how they behave and how you feel
2. Discuss in your small groups (of 4 or 5 people) and summarise these problems on flipchart paper
3. Post flipchart paper and present to other small groups in a total review. Seek and give clarification during this review, but do not pursue solutions at this point

The session was structured in a supportive way in order not to expose individuals and their problems to the total group.

PERSONALITY AND ATTITUDES OF CLIENTS AND THEIR REACTIONS TO CHANGE

At this point the concept of ego states was introduced using two exercises.

1 Two ego-state fantasies, similar to those in Chapter 12, one involving a high-power client, the other involving a

secretary (low-power). Both fantasies were related to the work of the advisers

2 Ego-state questionnaire (see Figure 14.7).

In conjunction with the exercises, the functional aspects of the ego states were described together with their behavioural characteristics, and two means of identifying them presented (behavioural and social). The positive and negative aspects were also explored, and contamination and exclusion outlined. In addition, the relationship was established between ego-state behaviour and the reactions of clients to change (see Figure 14.11).

Figure 14.11 Reactions to change

Adapted Child

Do nothing, avoid, forget
Get agitated, do a lot of things not very well
Get confused
Look for someone to take responsibility for them

Critical Parent

Angry
Hostile
Look for someone to 'kick'
May refuse to co-operate

'THE TYPES OF CLIENT I DEAL WITH'

At the end of the first day participants were asked to do an individual exercise overnight (see Figure 14.12). The aims of this overnight exercise were:

1 To provide a link to counter the effect of leaving and then returning to the training situation the next day.
2 To relate TA theory more closely to the situations the participants actually face.
3 To act as a basis for introducing the concepts of strokes and life positions.

RELATIONSHIPS WITH CLIENTS

The summaries derived from the exercise outlined in Figure 14.12

were discussed and used as a basis for introducing the concepts of strokes, life positions and transactions.

Figure 14.12 'The types of client I deal with'

> Individually, overnight, think about the types of client you deal with in terms of the learning so far (theory and practice)
>
> In the morning, meet in small groups for one hour and pick three examples of those who present the most difficulties
>
> Summarise, on flipchart:
> 1 their typical behaviour
> 2 your typical responses
> 3 the ego states involved

This was followed by a role play exercise very similar to the one shown in Figure 14.8, and designed to provide an opportunity for understanding transactions in greater depth. As with the ego-state fantasies, a low- and a high-power client are used in the 'scenes' to increase the chances of eliciting behaviour from all the ego states. After the exercise was carried out in small groups, the participants gathered together in the total group to discuss the experience.

DEALING WITH DIFFICULT CLIENTS

During the review of the previous exercise, the management of difficult relationships with clients was discussed, accompanied by two theoretical inputs: the choices available to an adviser for crossing transactions as discussed at the beginning of the chapter and the use of assertion techniques[4] as an additional aid for coping with stressful situations and maintaining self-worth. Four particular assertion techniques were discussed as follows:

1 The repeated statement of your position over and over again, in a calm relaxed (i.e. Adult) manner, enabling you to stick to your point without previous rehearsal of arguments or feelings
Examples: 'I sympathise with you, but there's nothing we can do about it.'
'Yes, I see your point of view, and I also think we need to see your boss to discuss it more fully.'

2 Calmly agreeing that there may be some basis to the criticism given, whilst remaining your own judge and avoiding fruitless arguments or feeling put down

Examples: 'You may be right there.'
'Yes, there's some truth in what you say.'

3 Firmly agreeing with criticism (whether hostile or helpful), without apologising, again avoiding arguments or feeling put down

Examples: 'You're absolutely right, we made a mistake.'
'Yes, I agree, I'm not very good at that.'

4 Actively seeking out criticism from a non-responsive client in order to expose it, and use it if helpful.

Examples: 'What things about our system don't you like?'
'Is there anything that I do that hinders you?'

UNDERSTANDING HIDDEN MESSAGES AND MANIPULATION BY CLIENTS

In this session a presentation on games was given, including:

what behaviours signal a game
what is happening at a transaction level
the drama triangle
examples of games, particularly those common in organisational and adviser/client relationships.

Participants were then asked to consider the games they got involved in with their clients by carrying out the exercise shown in Figure 14.13. The individual part of this activity was scheduled for overnight, again with the aim of providing some continuity, this time from the second to the third day.

On the third and final day, games with clients were reviewed and steps to avoid games considered.

EXPANDING RANGE OF SKILLS FOR USE IN ADVISING SITUATIONS – DEVELOPING COMMITMENT

Against a background of the difficulties involved in client–adviser relationships as examined from a TA viewpoint, time was then spent looking at the steps an adviser can take in developing commitment with his or her clients. Again, small group discussions were used to generate ideas, and a theory input made to synthesise and elaborate the learning, based on the list shown in Figure 14.14. Time structuring was also presented.

NEW WAYS OF DEALING WITH CLIENTS

In this final session, all the learning and problems discussed were reviewed to provide reinforcement, by small group discussion and total group review, and further choices developed for dealing with difficult situations.

ROLES OF THE STAFF IN THE ADVISING SKILLS COURSE FOR LIAISON GROUP ADVISERS

This particular programme provided an interesting issue about the roles and relationships of the course tutors – one external consultant

Figure 14.13 'Clients and their games'

1. Think of, and briefly describe, a situation where a client frequently:

   attempts to put you down
   exaggerates his own capacities and abilities
   puts himself down and exaggerates his own weaknesses
   sees you as manipulating him
   is always rushing around and too busy to see you

2. Think of a situation where you frequently find yourself offering advice and help
3. Spend ten minutes thinking about these situations, 1 and 2
4. In small groups, share and summarise on flipcharts
5. Review in total group

Figure 14.14 Some techniques for developing commitment

1. Give maximum number of benefits and payoffs
2. Give support and nurturing
3. Be straight about the problems and 'bad news'
4. Check agreements and understandings
   (e.g. 'Let's check where we've got to so far'
   'I see, so your position is . . .')
5. Use non-directive questions
   (e.g. 'Tell me more about . . .')
6. Actively listen and build on the client's data
7. Check the time available and clarify the agenda at the beginning of the meeting

acting as course leader supported by two internal trainers. Joint work involving external and internal professionals is a common feature of training, and may well be an increasing feature in the use of transactional analysis in organisations. In such a situation we have a four-cornered rather than a three-cornered contract (see Chapter 11), demanding steps to ensure even more clarity than usual in terms of responsibilities, practices, aims, etc. In this programme, the different training responsibilities of the staff involved were explicitly reviewed and agreed beforehand in terms of who was going to give theory inputs, present exercises, monitor small group discussions and lead review sessions. In addition, the fact that the internal trainers were to some degree also in a learning situation was recognised.

COMMENTS ON THE TWO ADVISING SKILLS PROGRAMMES

The second programme was a challenging one for a number of reasons, and brought sharply into focus the 'boundaries' of TA training in organisations, and interpersonal skills training generally (see Chapter 11). For example, the courses were structured on a '9-to-5' basis, non-residential, on the client's own premises (with all that entails in terms of the proximity of the organisational Parent, interruptions from work, etc.). There was also a fourth 'dimension' to the contract namely the internal–external trainer relationships as mentioned in the previous section. The participants themselves included many who were short on actual job experience and existing team relationships were never far away. TA clearly raised issues about these, but there was no contract to explore them. Whilst group discussions were generally effective, there was some resistance to role plays and dealing with here-and-now personal and group behaviour, despite some changes in the programme structure from the first to the second course. Nevertheless, a post-course questionnaire showed that most participants thought that the course was worthwhile and had helped them in their work.

As far as the first programme is concerned, there has been a general response of, first, an increase in felt level of confidence and, second, an increase in perceived range of choices and skills by participants at the end of the programme. The programme is continuing and an extensive review will be carried out in the near future. One final point. TA does throw some light on the relationship between the 'centre' of an organisation and the people at the boundary, such as training board advisers and salesmen (see Chapter 18). The problem for the 'centre' is getting information from the people at the boundary. Whether imagined or real, if the information flow to the 'Adult' at the centre is seen as inadequate, the risk is that the 'Child' at the centre gets scared or agitated. All too typically, the response is to switch to Parent and increase the control and limitations placed on those 'out in the field'. This in turn often hooks rebellion or delay from the Adapted Child ego state, and a vicious circle is set up. This is an organisational development problem, where the missing ingredient is trust.

REFERENCES

1 See W.G. Bennis, K.D. Benne and R. Chin, *The Planning of Change*, Holt, Rinehart and Winston, 1969.
Also F. Friedlander, 'OD reaches adolescence' and W. Burke, 'OD in transition' in *Journal of Applied Behavioural Science*, vol. 12, no. 1, 1976.
2 C. Argyris, *Intervention Theory and Method; a Behavioural Science View*, Addison-Wesley, 1970.
3 D. Jongeward and M. James, *Winning with People; Group Exercises in TA*, Addison-Wesley, 1973.
4 M.J. Smith, *When I Say No, I Feel Guilty*, The Dial Press, 1975.

15 TA, organisation development and team building

ORGANISATION DEVELOPMENT (OD)

Organisation development[1] is the planned intervention into an organisation's activity and existence with the aims of helping the organisation:

respond to existing internal and external pressures for change
meet future pressures for change
increase its effectiveness in carrying out its business.

Typically, this planned intervention may be made at one or more of four points:

1 The resources the organisation uses (both material and human)
2 The systems adopted for meeting the goals of the organisation (e.g. accounting, administrative and personnel procedures)
3 The structures employed (e.g. the company hierarchy and formal roles within it)
4 The culture and relationships between the people working in the organisation.

These four domains are not discrete by any means, and, as OD practitioners know only too well, intervention in any one is likely to have repercussions for the others. Typically, OD is carried out with the help of external agents, but not necessarily, and increasingly personnel departments are becoming the centre for such practice,[2] particularly under the impact of employment legislation.

As far as intervention at the level of relationships is concerned, one significant approach has been the T-group and all its derivatives, though there have been some significant exceptions to this (e.g., behaviour analysis,[3] and, more recently, Gestalt.[4]) Currently, TA presents itself as an additional approach for use in organisation development, and this chapter presents some ideas as to how it is, and how it might be, used for this.

TA IN ORGANISATION DEVELOPMENT

The application of TA in organisation development raises some important concerns. TA is in many senses 'counter-culture' (see p.90) to the existing beliefs and standards of our organisations. Even the possibility of looking at how 'I' relate to 'you' is taboo to some, let alone the idea of 'I' expressing anger or fear.

The obvious point of application of TA is at the level of relationships in the organisation, although it does have implications for structure, systems and resources. For example, many of our organisations are characterised to a lesser or greater degree by exploitation not only of people but also of the environment in the service of industrial and economic growth. They have grown in size and complexity by taking this position but TA confronts this exploitation. Consequently, its widespread use may have consequence for the way in which we structure our organisations.

TA AS A TOOL FOR IMPROVING INTERPERSONAL RELATIONSHIPS

The basis for the work described in Chapters 12, 13 and 14 is the use of TA as a tool for improving interpersonal skills in specific situations. Whilst the use of TA in such situations may constitute only a minimal effort in OD terms, it does have a general applicability for the development of interpersonal skills. One particularly important area of application is team building, using TA to improve the relationships in an existing organisational team or department (see pages 160–162, and also Chapter 16). Intervention at the level of team building and team relationships is one of the most effective approaches to developing organisations and has become a major OD strategy.[5] Further, it allows the direct and explicit use of TA as an aid to process consultation. Process consultation[6] is the on-line intervention of a consultant into the behaviour of a work group (as opposed to off-site training) – for example, comments on the behaviour of a group and its members by the consultant, while the group is having a routine meeting to discuss its business. If such a group is familiar with TA and has developed awareness and trust in themselves and trust in a consultant through a team building programme, then TA can be used for process consulting (see Chapter 16).

TA AS AN APPROACH TO EXAMINE THE CLIENT–OD CONSULTANT RELATIONSHIP (see also Chapter 14)

OD practitioners have identified the relationship between OD consultant and client as a key dynamic in organisation change processes.[7] This point has been taken up by Novey (who makes some general comments on TA and organisational change in his book[8]). He pro-

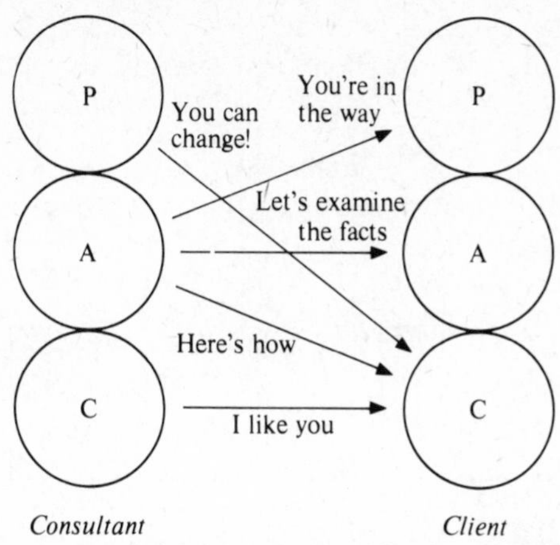

Figure 15.1 Client–consultant transactions in change

poses that the client–consultant relationship can be viewed in TA terms as show in Figure 15.1.

The consultant aims to give 'permission' from his/her Parent to the Child of the client that change is possible ('You can change!') and backs this up by developing with the client ways to change (Adult to Child message, 'Here's how'). The Adult of the consultant also works with the client's Adult to diagnose the problems around ('Let's examine the facts') and gives feedback on those values and practices that are interfering with constructive change (Adult to Parent message, 'You're in the way'). Finally, for the work to be effective, there has to be a basis of mutual trust and support (Child to Child message, 'I like you').

THE USE OF TA CONCEPTS AT A GROUP AND ORGANISATIONAL LEVEL

TA concepts, though essentially personal and interpersonal, can be 'extrapolated' to a group and organisational level. The concept of Parent itself, and transactions between Parent and Child, gives us an important way of looking at authority issues in organisations, Taking this a step further, for example, it is possible to describe the style of authority used in an organisation in egogram terms (Chapter 2), to an approximation (Figure 15.2). As shown, the model also proposes how this authority base might be changed in the same terms.

The egogram shows a decrease in Critical Parent with a corresponding decrease in Adapted Child behaviour, and an increase in Adult, Nurturing Parent and Free Child behaviour. (It might be possible to

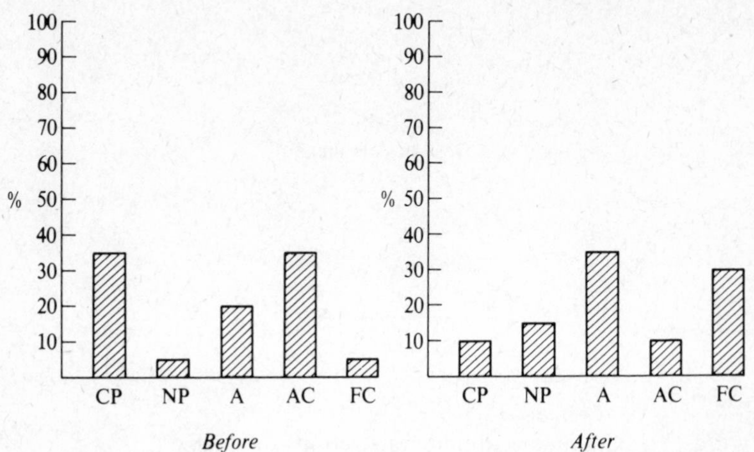

Figure 15.2 Egogram of an organisation before and after planned change

diagnose the change with selected questionnaires, or direct observation, together with the subjective impressions of those involved.) Similarly, such concepts as life positions and strokes can be used to describe the present culture of an organisation and suggest how it might be following an organisation development intervention.

SCRIPTS AND ORGANISATION DEVELOPMENT

Organisational scripts have been referred to in Chapter 9, and offer a potent approach to looking at change in organisations. Male and female scripts[9] and their differences are also important influences on organisational behaviour. Male scripting, with its emphasis on Critical Parent behaviour and the adoption of roles by organisational members based on power and achievement, predominates in organisations, as portrayed in Figure 15.3.

The current demand that seems to be developing for organisations to focus on the quality of their internal relationships and to change them in the direction of greater democracy and authenticity, in turn demands a reduction in the influence of these injunctions and an increase in the influence of behaviours more usually identified as female scripting, e.g. caring, sharing, openness to feelings, intuition, closeness, etc. In short, the ideas of male scripts, female scripts and organisational scripts give us a means to look at whole cultures, their values and the problems of change they have to cope with.[10]

Figure 15.3 Injunctions in organisations arising from male scripts

Don't lose control
Don't ask for help
Never be satisfied
Don't settle for second best
Don't trust
Don't feel
Don't show your feelings
Don't let the others beat you (be competitive)
Don't let the others put you down (put them down first)
Don't admit you're wrong

TA AND OD CONCEPTS

Organisation development practitioners have developed many models over the years of examining and explaining their work, and these models can be interpreted in TA terms. For example a frequent and widely use idea for looking at change is shown in Figure 15.4, together with the associated ego states.

Figure 15.4 Ego states in the process of change

Change is possible where:

	(1) dissatisfaction with the present	(Critical Parent and Adapted Child)
plus	(2) a vision of the future	(Adult and Free Child)
plus	(3) some practical first steps	(Adult and Nurturing Parent)
outweigh	(4) the fear of changing	(Critical Parent and Adapted Child)

TA AND THEORIES OF MANAGEMENT

Running parallel with the growth of organisation development since the war has been the development of numerous approaches to management behaviour and the improvement of management effectiveness. As noted by other authors,[8,11] TA integrates with, supports and adds to such theories as:

McGregor's 'theory X and Y'
Blake and Mouton's 'managerial grid'
Likert's 'four systems of management'
Herzberg's 'motivation–hygiene' theory
Argyris's 'maturity–immaturity' theory
Drucker's 'management by objectives' approach.

Further TA does not appear to detract from or conflict with them in any significant way. The implication of this is that TA can be introduced into organisations together with or following the introduction of such approaches as a natural step in their development.

TA AND TEAM BUILDING

WHAT IS TEAM BUILDING?

One of the main problems in any form of social skills training is retention. More specifically, whatever significant personal learning an individual gets from a course and whatever changes in behaviour that individual successfully experiments with, the impact of the learning frequently fades with time. There are some reasons for this. There is often insufficient support in the organisation for applying the new learning. Many significant individuals interacting with the one-time course member have an investment in the participant staying as he was (so as to play their favourite games, for example).

Another problem is that some participants gain increased self-confidence, greater awareness of their own capacities and skills, and greater understanding of the ways they have given their power away to others. As a consequence, they no longer 'fit' the job demands nor the behaviour demands of others and consequently may take the step of finding another job.

To overcome these kinds of problems, which were particularly noted during the early use of T-groups, the 1950s and 1960s saw the development of team building as a training and OD intervention into organisations. Team building is a planned intervention aimed at developing the skills of workgroups (doing interrelated jobs) in goal achievement through improving the ways used by the group of goal setting and of interacting with each other. It involves some kind of training activity, together with data gathering, consultation and review sessions. These activities usually fall into three phases:

data gathering and preparation
team development workshop(s)
follow-up and integration.

Figure 15.5 Typical aims of team building and related aspects of behaviour in TA terms

Typical goals	*TA concepts*
Increase clarity of goals	Increase use of Adult ego state and 'straightness' of transactions
Increase commitment to goals and sense of team identity	Increase Free Child, exchange of positive strokes and intimacy
Clarify roles and responsibilities	Increase use of Adult ego state and 'straightness' of transactions
Introduce skills in examining behaviour and its consequences	Increase use of Adult ego state
Increase openness of communication	Increase intimacy
Improve effectiveness of decison-making process	Increase use of Adult ego state and 'straightness' of transactions
Increase skill at handling change	Increase use of Adult ego state
Increase skill at learning from experience	Increase use of Adult ego state
Increase level of trust and mutual concern	Increase use of Free Child, Nurturing Parent, exchange of positive strokes and intimacy
Increase creativity and contributions	Increase Free Child and use of Adult ego state

Typical groups for team building include permanent departments and teams, temporary teams, such as project groups and working parties, and even staff representation bodies. It is unusual for there to be more than three levels of hierarchy involved, but the members of the team will have interrelated jobs.

AIMS OF TEAM BUILDING

The specific aims involved for a given team building programme are very much a question of agreement between the parties concerned. Figure 15.5 shows a list of some typical aims (which overlap) and their interpretation in TA terms. The TA concepts are shown in terms of increases. As a corollary to these increases, there would be a decrease in Critical Parent, Adapted Child, negative strokes, games and stamp collecting, for example.

Based on these aims, TA offers itself as a significant resource for team building programmes. The next section outlines its use in a TA-based team building programme carried out across the management structure of an organisation. Chapter 16 describes in detail the use of TA in a team building programme together with approaches derived from the T-group arena.

TA AT EDWARDS HIGH VACUUM

THE SETTING AND THE NEED

This section describes how TA was introduced in a high technology company employing 1100 people in southern England, Edwards High Vacuum.[12] The Board of the company had developed a charter for human relations, whose objective was to produce a more participative management style. TA was chosen as an appropriate training technique to help this organisational change because it provides a framework which:

1 Has a high cognitive content and is therefore suitable for skilled, technically qualified staff
2 Can be used to analyse individual behaviour and personality
3 Has an easily understood language
4 Has a low risk of adverse effects on the organisation.

A formal presentation was made to the Board and approval obtained for ten workshops of 2½-days' duration, involving twelve to fifteen participants and two trainers. The workshops were not therefore strictly speaking team building courses in the sense that the participants on each one all came from a single department or unit, but rather were taken from across the management structure of the organisation as a whole.

AIMS OF THE WORKSHOPS

The workshops had three objectives:

1 To increase manager's awareness of their management style and its effect on others
2 To provide managers with a framework to develop and improve their working relationships
3 To encourage a more participative style

CONTENT OF THE WORKSHOPS

After the introductory session a particular feature of the first evening was that it was used to identify work problems which participants were currently facing. Having identified them they were then encouraged to resolve them during the workshop using the TA framework. This emphasis on relating concepts to 'real problems' was a very significant aspect of the workshop.

The second day was used to acquaint participants with the basic TA concepts of ego states, transactions time structuring and strokes. The trainers experienced a problem with which other trainers are probably familiar: loss of energy by participants in the late afternoon. They overcame this very successfully by introducting fifteen minutes of simple relaxation and breathing exercises.

In the early workshops participants had difficulties grasping the concept of 'games'. The trainers resolved this by leading into games via ulterior transactions, reinforced by role playing activities in small groups. The final part of the workshop was spent in drawing-up individual action plans, which participants were encouraged to implement when back at work. A review session was held two weeks after the workshop to give feedback to the trainers. This helped them modify certain aspects of the workshop (e.g. handling of games).

Overall, the programme has been very successful. The tutors are aware of its limitations (e.g. as a tool for developing group effectiveness) but are satisfied that it has substantially helped to develop more effective working relationships. This view has been endorsed by many of the participants.

SOME COMMENTS

Two significant features of the workshops are the integration of TA with an opportunity for the participants to resolve their own work problems and the use of relaxation and breathing exercises for participants to regain their energy in the late afternoon sessions.

The TA workshops are not the only strategies for achieving the goal of producing a more participative management style. Other steps taken include shop floor involvement in the layout of machines and the use of briefing groups for the disclosure of financial information. TA is thus being used as one element in a total organisational change programme.

REFERENCES

1 W.G. Bennis, K.D. Benne and R. Chin, *The Planning of Change*, Holt, Rinehart and Winston, 1969.
2 M. Thakur, 'OD; the search for identity', *Information Report* no. 16, Institute of Personnel Management, 1974.
3 N. Rackman and T. Morgan, *Behavioural Analysis in Training*, McGraw-Hill, 1977.
4 S.M. Herman and M. Korenich, *Authentic Management: A Gestalt Orientation to Organisations and their Development*, Addison-Wesley, 1977.
5 E. Frank and C. Margerison, 'Training methods and organisation development', *Journal of European and Industrial Training*, vol. 2, no. 4, 1978.
6 E.H. Schein, *Process Consultation: Its Role in Organisation Development*, Addison-Wesley, 1969.
7 C. Argyris, *Intervention Theory and Method: A Behavioural Science View*, Addison-Wesley, 1970.
8 T.B. Novey, *TA for Management*, Jalmar Press Inc., 1976.
9 C.M. Steiner, *Scripts People Live*, Grove Press Inc., 1974.
10 T. White and J.D. White, 'The implications of cultural scripting' in *TA After Eric Berne*, G. Barnes (ed), Harpers College Press, 1977.
11 D. Jongeward et al. *Everybody Wins: TA Applied to Organisations*, Addison-Wesley, 1973.
12 M. Wellin, 'TA in the workplace,' *Personnel Management*, July 1978.

16 TA in a team building programme

This chapter outlines the development of a team building programme for a specialist group in an industrial training board. It highlights some of the challenges, dilemmas and complexities involved in defining the learning needs and choosing the appropriate technology for such a programme, and demonstrates the interface between TA and organisation development.

THE SETTING

The group involved in the programme is a specialist consulting team in the board. The group is responsible for offering advice largely of a financial and operational nature to small clients covered by the training board concerned. Most of the team operate in pairs (one a financial expert and one an operational) in defined regional areas. Their work is based on a cycle of activities as follows:

1 Diagnosis (by visits and discussions) of the needs of a group of clients in a geographical area
2 Training presentations based on these needs
3 Post-training review and consultation
4 Repeat of the process in a new area.

They consequently have rather temporary relationships with their clients as opposed to the more permanent situation that many training board advisers face; in fact their work involves liaison with the field training board advisers responsible for the areas concerned. The team consisted of one manager and fourteen advisers and saw themselves as an elite group within the organisation. They were geographically dispersed, meeting on average once a month as a group. Although consultancy was the nature of their work and interpersonal skills an important aspect of this, they shared with the organisation as a whole a scepticism of external consultants and social and interpersonal skills training (not without reason as there had been some unhappy past experiences).

THE INITIAL NEED

An initial meeting with the internal staff development adviser of the board established some broad needs. He had been involved in some work with the team on training technology and presentation techniques. This contact had thrown up a number of issues:

1 Concerns about interpersonal skills
2 Concerns about, and resistance to, changes (some of the changes were being initiated by the manager, and some imposed from outside the team)
3 While the team members were performing well in their consulting role, there were concerns about low commitment to the team as a whole.

The staff development adviser had made a commitment to establish what kind of learning/training would resolve these issues.

FURTHER DIAGNOSIS AND CLARIFICATION OF AIMS

There then followed two meetings with the internal staff development adviser and the manager of the team. At the first meeting the three important relationship dimensions of the team were clarified as being:

1 1 : 1 (client consulting) } external
2 1 to group (training of groups of clients) } relationships

3 internal team relationships

The problems in these relationships were summarised as:

lack of self-confidence in training sessions
lack of self-confidence in in-company consulting
negative attitudes to change
lack of vision as to potential for growth of self and client
competition between pairs
resistance to mutual support in the team as a whole.

At this point an agreement was reached to use a training programme to deal with these problems and to consider and establish options for such a programme.

There are important issues relevant to this stage of the work:

1 During this phase much time was spent with the staff development adviser and manager, not only to clarify facts and needs and establish goals and methods but also as part of the overall trust and credibility building that is required in any team development work. In other words, investing time saves time and even prevents disaster. Certainly, the manager of any group

involved in team building requires considerable support because their authority, role and style is almost always a focal issue

2 There was a potential credibility and integration issue because the training technology and assumptions about learning experienced by the team both in the trainer and the trainee role was dissonant with that used in interpersonal skills training and team building. This issue did in fact raise itself during the team building workshop

3 At this point it was unclear as to whether the prime focus of the workshop should be team relationships or client relationships, or whether to attempt a mix of the two. It was decided that a mixed focus could be attempted and a preliminary programme was developed as shown in Figure 16.1. However the appropriate technology was clearly a cycle of theory, experience and review (with theory emphasised particularly in phase two of the programme) based on a portfolio of options to meet emerging group needs, rather than a rigid trainer-orientated structure. This flexibility would be important particularly towards the end of the week as the focus on feedback and personal learning intensified

4 Transactional analysis was emerging as a suitable technology to use on the programme. The team were geographically dispersed with relatively low interdependency, only meeting occasionally as a group. Consequently, TA, unlike group dependent frameworks, would have a direct contribution to make not only to their operating pairs but also to their client relationships (both 1 : 1 and training presentations). It would probably make the integration between the consulting relationships and the team relationships areas of the workshop easier. Finally, there was some uncertainty about the future structure and even existence of the team. In the event of organisational changes, it seemed likely that team members would have the opportunity to transfer the learning to new situations more easily with TA than with group-dependent approaches

5 It was clear that whatever aims were developed in response to the needs and problems outlined earlier, participants were likely to gain greater awareness of self and others almost as a by-product. As stated, the nature of authority in the team was also likely to be confronted. Some of the problems outlined in themselves raised secondary difficulties. Take for example 'negative attitudes to change'. It is certainly not the consultant's role in this situation to 'sell' the demands and plans for change by senior management to such a group, nor would it be productive in relation to the other issues (e.g. 'resistance to mutual support in

Figure 16.1 Preliminary programme

Phase	*Learning vehicles/aim*	*Time*
Introductory	Opening exercises to promote orientation to situation	½ day
Learning a shared model of behaviour	TA concepts plus exercises	1 day
Application 1	Client relationships	1–1½ days
Application 2	Team relationships	1–1½ days
Closing	Back-home planning to integrate and transfer aspects of week's learning to organisational situation	½ day

the team as a whole'). On the other hand, effective team development workshops can resolve the issue of change and the ownership of change by supporting feedback, confrontation, openness, delegation and joint goal planning

6 At least part of the programme was to be orientated to team development. As a consequence an essential requirement was to gather data from the rest of the team, and build up trust and credibility with them, not just the manager. The use of questionnaires for this task does have the advantage of getting information from everyone concerned but can sometimes increase mistrust and 'distance' potential participants before any substantial work has started. Interviewing in depth a random sample of the participants seemed a better alternative

7 As well as those concerns and potential outcomes present in any social and interpersonal skill training situation (e.g. overspill of learning to non-work situations, divergent nature of learning, potential for resistance and rejection by some participants, raising of personal issues for some participants demanding post-course counselling), team building raises three others. First, the team may well increase its sense of 'OK-ness' about itself and the euphoric experience that often occurs with such a programme may be accompanied by a sense of others as being 'not OK'. This may lead to problems of communication with other parts of the organisation (or alternatively 'we want some of that training' as a

response from others). Second, in team building programmes operational and structural issues are likely to be raised which require attention by senior management if the programme is to maintain its effectiveness. Third, team building usually involves feedback and this raises particular issues for authority figures. Care is required to support the giving of feedback on the one hand and the acceptance and utilisation of it on the other. In some ways, team building is more of a risk for the manager than it is the subordinate as it involves removing the defence of status.

At the second meeting all these issues were reviewed, including trust building and credibility, the aims of the training, the design and nature of the training, and potential outcomes. While there were some reservations about using TA, the preliminary programme model (Figure 16.1) was agreed together with the need to use a flexible and largely experiential approach. The aims of the programme were agreed as in Figure 16.2 and a letter drafted to workshop participants for reasons referred to in previous chapters. No mention of TA was made at this stage. Arrangements were made for the manager to hold a special meeting with his team and gauge the extent of support for the programme. While some scepticism and doubts were expressed at this meeting there was general support for continuing with the programme.

PRE-COURSE INTERVIEWS

Six members of the team were selected at random without any prior knowledge about their views and attitudes, and interviewed for approximately one-and-a-half hours by the staff involved in the programme. The interviews were performed on a 1:1 basis. The goals of the interviews are as listed in Figure 16.3, whilst Figure 16.4 gives a list of typical questions asked during these interviews. In order to meet the goals listed in Figure 16.3 a fairly non-directive style was used, the interviewers talking less than 25 per cent of the time, using the questions in Figure 16.4 as a basis. The questions were not asked in any particular order, not all of them were asked and new ones introduced according to the emerging needs.

Much data had already been gathered from the manager directly and indirectly. Six interviews out of a possible fourteen is only sufficient to give data for confirmation or otherwise of the workshop going ahead, and for general information on design. (In a more orthodox organisation development programme, all the participants might be interviewed and the data produced used as material to work on in the programme.)

Figure 16.2 Aims of the team building programme

To develop self-confidence in both client training and in-company consulting situations

To develop more positive attitudes to change

To develop greater awareness of own and client's potential

To reduce level of competition between pairs

To increase the level of mutual support and 'levelling' between pairs

These aims may require modification or extension as a result of the interviews. In working towards these aims, three other outcomes are likely:

(a) increased self-awareness
(b) increased awareness of others
(c) exploration and understanding of authority relationships and issues

Figure 16.3 Goals of the interviews

To gather information on the group's culture, ways of doing things, ways of relating, and impact of roles on individuals and individuals on roles

To gather information of group and individual issues, problems, difficulties, frustrations, hopes and aspirations

To gather information on the interpersonal style of some members of the group on the basis of their interaction with the interviewers

To give people an opportunity to question the interviewer and work on any beliefs or stereotypes they may have about him

To develop acceptance of the interviewers in preparation for further work

To gather data to refine the design of the workshop, or alternatively to discover if there is any data suggesting the workshop should not go ahead

Figure 16.4 Basic questions for interviews

Tell me briefly about your personal and career background prior to taking up the job you are doing now

How do you see your current job?

What are the challenges and frustrations in your job?

How does your job influence your behaviour?

Do you think you are using all your resources and capabilities in your job?

What issues or problems do you come across in the training situation?

What issues or problems do you come across in the consulting situation?

Do you see yourself having to operate differently in the different situations and does this pose any problem?

How do you judge your success at your job?

What do you see as being your strengths? What do you see as being areas for your development?

What do you see as your next step in terms of development?

Where do you see yourself in ten years time?

What are you going to do to get there?

Do you see yourself in a changing situation?

How do you respond to change?

What do you think of your clients?

What do you do if you get an awkward client, who, for example, won't co-operate/avoids doing things/tries to push you around?

Who are the most important people to you in your job?

How important are good relationships to you in your job?

What do you think constitutes a good working relationship?

Do you see yourself as a member of a team; if so what is it?

What are your views on the way the team operates?

What improvements do you think would be good for the group either technically or in terms of its operating style?

What do you want to get from the workshop?

What do you want to see happen at the workshop?

The interviews highlighted some important issues and brought out some opposing viewpoints and attitudes. At the same time they did not contra-indicate the running of a workshop for the team. Some of the key issues included:

1 The manager's position had not been formalised, leading to uncertainties about his responsibilities and authority
2 Uncertainty about the future of the group existed and change was anticipated by some (e.g. break-up and/or amalgamation). Some interviewees thought this would be useful, others not, favouring a consolidation of the group
3 Judged by one important criterion, the group was barely a team: there was low interdependence, even among work pairs. They were not dependent on one another to any significant extent for performing their job except in the case of special projects or new development work. There was also low interaction with the other parts of the organisation. Yet the proposal to run a workshop clearly implied that there was a team. The value of the team seemed to be in the personal and professional support they could give one another rather than in the task. At any rate, this data confirmed the use of TA rather than a group-based approach as a significant input
4 The team comprised a small 'in-group', close to the manager and involved in changes and new developments, and a larger 'out-group'. This presented an inter-group dimension and was the crux of the 'negative attitudes to change' issue
5 On the other hand some of the working pairs (though not all) seemed to offer a good deal of mutual support, contrary to the initial picture given
6 Approaches to the task varied considerably from the routine and precedent-bound to the highly innovative (even against the wishes of the manager)
7 For some, the job was experienced as 'lonely' and very low in strokes with little contact with colleagues, the organisation as a whole and only temporary contact with the clients. The constant cycle of setting up training presentations with groups of clients and then terminating the relationships gave constant separation issues.

Consideration of this data shows different weights of importance to the aims (Figure 16.2) of decreasing competition and increasing mutual support between pairs as far as the participants were concerned, and also highlights the whole issue of responsibility for and attitudes to change as a key issue. The organisational and structural uncertainties clearly placed limitations on the potential gains from the workshop and there was still a dilemma between client relationships and team relationships as a focus (Figure 16.5, boxes 4 and 5) with consequences for the programme design. Focusing on intrapersonal, interpersonal and authority relationships (Figure 16.5, boxes 1,2 and 3) seemed appropriate to most of the aims with potential benefits for team effectiveness and was congruent with the use of TA. It also seemed likely that any increased sense of self-confidence and power developed at both the individual and group level could be used by the team to deal with team-organisation issues, e.g. resolution of structural uncertainties. With these points in mind, the preliminary programme outlined in Figure 16.1 still seemed appropriate but with the proviso that much flexibility would be needed to respond to the team's needs with respect to a client or team relationships focus.

These issues were discussed at a final meeting with the manager and staff development adviser prior to the commencement of the programme. Despite the uncertainties about the direction the workshop would take, an outline programme was sent to all participants, based on the final programme shown in Figure 16.6.

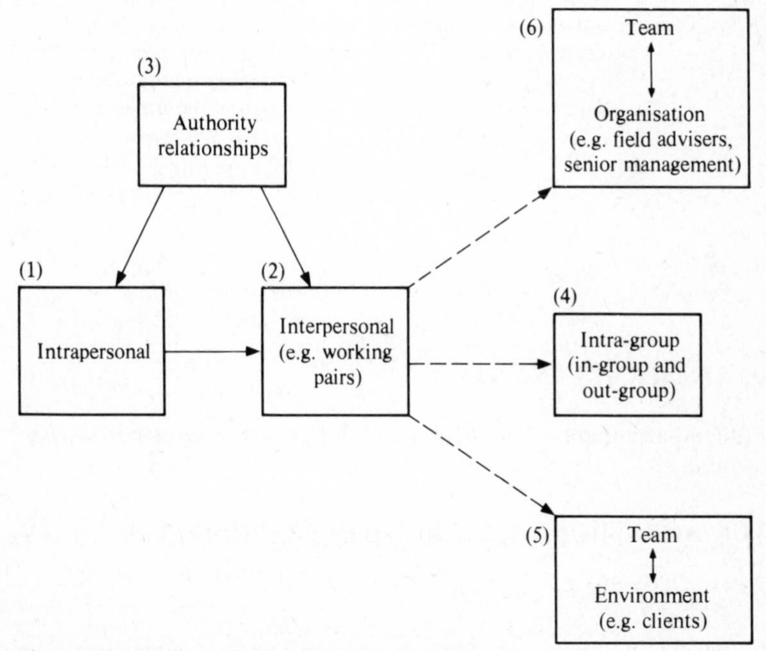

Figure 16.5 Focus for workshop activities

Figure 16.6 Final programme

Phase	*Activities*	*Aims*
1 *Introductory phase*	Exchange of expectations and workshop aims 'Three things I like about myself' exercise	Clarify nature and business of week Orientate to situation
2 *Self-learning phase*	Learning a shared model of behaviour, TA, using theory inputs and exercises	Language and concepts familiarisation Building trust in situation. Developing openness Increasing understanding and awareness about self and others
3 *Self and task phase*	Exercise and theory on consulting relationships	Use of learning in relation to primary task. Bridge-building to deeper levels of personal and group work
4 *Self and group phase*	Team building activities and exercises, with high emphasis on feedback and goal clarification	Resolving interpersonal and authority conflicts Decrease competition, increasing mutual support and group commitment, increase sense of power over own destiny and influence over change processes
5 *Closing phase*	Final exercise(s)	Integrate and transfer workshop learning to organisational situation

PARTICIPANTS AND STAFF

Fifteen participants were involved in the workshop together with two training staff.

THE WORKSHOP (AN EXERCISE IN TRAINING FLEXIBILITY)

INTRODUCTORY PHASE

Following personal introductions, aims and expectations were reviewed and discussed in the total group as outlined in Figure 16.2 and the pre-course letter. At this point a good deal of hostility was expressed by the participants towards the situation, but there was a general willingness to proceed. Five trios were then self-chosen (with the ground rule that they did not include current working partners) to discuss 'three things I like about myself' (Figure 16.7). The aim of this was to introduce the group to the personal and largely experiential nature of the workshop including the giving of feedback and expression of feelings and to encourage an increase in sense of self worth. (Some of the participants found this self-stroking difficult. This simple exercise often highlights this difficulty; see the idea of 'stroke economy' in Chapter 3).

SELF-LEARNING PHASE

Using the previous exercise as a basis, the concept of strokes was introduced. Working in the same trios as before, participants filled out stroke profiles (see Chapter 3) and discussed their implications with their colleagues.

Figure 16.7 'Three things I like about myself' exercise

Form trios, not including your working partner

Share in your trio three things you like about yourself, in terms of your behaviour, i.e. what you *do*

Report how you feel when you share these 'three things'

Get feedback on how the other members of your trio felt when you stated your 'three things'

Ego states were then introduced (together with exclusion and contamination) using an ego-state fantasy exercise similar to the one in Chapter 14 but adapted to the team's operating circumstances.

At this point (the end of the first day) a number of issues had arisen about the workshop:

1 Expressions of suspicion about what the staff were doing
2 Concern about the openness required in the exercises (clearly a very new experience for some of the participants)
3 Avoidance of meaningful work in some trios
4 Expression of dependency ('Tell us what's right or wrong') from an Adapted Child position
5 Expressions of counter-dependency (hostility towards staff) from a rebellious Adapted Child and Critical Parent position
6 Doubt about the credibility of the staff (lack of terminal

behaviour objectives in orthodox training terms plus reflexive and open-ended style of trainers)

7 Concerns about implications of TA (e.g. comments like 'If you choose which ego stage to respond from, don't you lose your humanness and spontaneity?').

It thus appeared that the phases of dependency and counter-dependency that occur in T-group training were emerging in this situation also.[1]

On day two, participants were encouraged to complete a personal diary (see Chapter 17), with the aim of focusing their concerns and needs, and also of providing a post-workshop record. This activity was repeated at the start of each day.

The concepts of transactions, games, life positions and time structuring were next introduced, together with the drama triangle exercise, Figure 16.8. The introduction of this exercise proved to be very important in terms of facilitating the expression of feedback not only in the exercise trios but also between individuals in the total group. This was supported by the staff, who also gave their feedback to individuals, either reflexively (i.e. 'What I experience when you do that') and/or interpretatively (using the descriptions of behaviour provided by TA).

A clear issue had now emerged about the listening skills of the group, exacerbated by its relatively large size (fifteen), and the tendency for feedback to be resisted rather than received and explored. On this basis, the listening skills exercise shown in Figure 16.9 was introduced. The group was divided in two for this activity, each with one member of staff to maintain the ground rules. While the prime aim was to focus on and improve listening skills, the task set also had the aim of focusing the participants on which of two areas was the important one for them – client relationships or team relationships.

SELF AND TASK PHASE

This phase commenced with a request to the group to self-select three groups of five for a practical activity. This self-selection of small groups was deliberate and aimed at sharing the reponsibility of the workshop with the group. However, there was considerable difficulty experienced in carrying out this self-selection. It was eventually resolved by one member of the group initiating by drawing up three lists of small groups and the group then proceeded with the activity. However, it became clear that as far as the majority of the group were concerned, this phase was not meaningful, and team relationships and goals were seen as the relevant business to proceed with. The staff then called a halt to this phase, kept the participants in the same groups (of five) and moved on to the next phase.

Figure 16.8 Drama triangle exercise

1 *Exercise*
 (a) Divide into small groups of three
 (b) Allocate the three roles of persecutor, victim and rescuer between the three of you
 (c) Persecutor starts by criticising the victim about anything, e.g. colour of tie, coming in late to the session, not contributing to the session, etc.
 (d) Rescuer and victim then respond freely, and trio allow transactions to proceed, each attempting to stay in their allocated drama triangle position
 (e) After a few minutes, change roles, pick different subjects, and start again

2 *Review*
 (a) Do you find yourself moving around the triangle, i.e. starting in one position, then moving to another?
 (b) Do you always end up in the same drama triangle position wherever you start?

Figure 16.9 Exercise in listening skills

The group is to hold a discussion for 35 minutes on the following topic:

> 'Relationships in the group have little to do with relationships in the field'

The group will divide into two separate subgroups for this activity and operate according to the following groundrules:

1 Each subgroup will be given a pen
2 Only one person can speak at once
3 That person must be holding the pen
4 You may not ask for, or signal for, the pen
5 If you are given the pen you must repeat the last 10 words of the person who handed you the pen
6 When you have the pen you may not keep it longer than two minutes
7 You may give the pen to whoever you choose

SELF AND GROUP PHASE

Group-level role negotiation

The group were then asked to carry out a group-level modification of Harrison's role negotiation exercise[2] as shown in Figure 16.10. This had a number of consequences:

1 Establishing and clarifying the group's goals
2 Focusing the problem areas for the group, both task and interpersonal
3 Clearing up fantasies and rumours about changes in the group
4 Putting the in-group out-group issue 'on the table'.

It also signalled an end to aggressive or avoiding behaviour towards the task of the workshop, and the acceptance of the staff as a resource with specific skills to contribute to that task.

Figure 16.10 Group-level role negotiation

In small groups of five, list your views under the following headings:

1 'What can the group do more of or start doing?'
2 'What can the group do less of or stop doing?'
3 'What can the group continue to do same of?'

in order to maintain and increase its effectiveness

Group problem-solving skills

At this point the group spent some time developing problem-solving skills based on its emerging sense of collaboration and commitment. One of the problem areas identified in the previous activity was chosen and a 'brainstorming' session[3] used to produce alternatives for resolving it. In TA terms, brainstorming involves the separation of Child inventiveness and creativity (the ideas and alternatives generating stage) from Adult reality testing and Parent value checking (the judging phase). While brainstorming does lead to novel high-quality solutions to problems, by reducing interference from external 'active' Parent judgements, participants may still be inhibited by internal 'influencing' Parent messages (i.e. the individual contributor dismisses his/her contribution through a rapid internal dialogue and put-down). It seems probable that, in an atmosphere of heightened awareness and trust developed in a team building programme, this is less likely to happen. Certainly there was a lot of Free Child expressed by the group during this activity as demonstrated by the expression of humour and fun.

Total group meeting

On the fourth day, the group continued to resolve the in-group/out-group issues and increased its level of interpersonal feedback with the support of the staff. Several groundrules were reinforced by the staff to aid this process as shown in Figure 16.11. (These groundrules show the influence of T-group, TA and Gestalt thinking on learning processes). The groundrules have the aim of increasing assertiveness, self-responsibility and personal power while reducing aggression, hostility and defensive behaviour, as well as supporting the development of group cohesion, commitment and establishing interpersonal behaviour as a legitimate focus for the group.

This session was marked by a distinct change in behaviour of the group, as signified by:

a willingness to listen
a reduction in preparation of responses while someone else was talking
a reduction in interruptions
a reduction in 'yes . . . but . . .' statements as compared with the earlier part of the workshops.

However, there was still a tendency to avoid levelling and direct confrontation.

Figure 16.11 Groundrules for feedback

1. Rather than judging the other person, state what the other person does and what you think, feel and do in response
2. Ask for clarification and specific examples where appropriate when given feedback
3. Listen to the feedback, rather than defending
4. Own what you say. Say 'I' rather than 'we', 'they', 'one', 'you'
5. Own your own feelings. Say 'In response to what you do, I feel . . .', rather than 'You make me feel . . .'
6. Focus on behaviour (what a person does) rather than personality (what a person is)
7. Don't tell people 'What you should do . . .'

Subgroup feedback session

In order to intensify the levelling and confrontation in a supportive way, the group split into two and continued the feedback according to the directions in Figure 16.12, without contributions from the staff. Note that the negative strokes were expressed before the positive ones.

Figure 16.12 Feedback subgroups

1 Draw up a list for each colleague in your subgroup of:

   (a) 'Two things you do that I don't like'
   (b) 'Two things you do that I do like'

2 Take it in turn to receive this feedback, 'don't likes' first

Closing phase

On the final day, the group used a shortened version of Harrison's role negotiations exercise[2] to finalise individual contracts about behaviour change, based on the feedback developed in the previous sessions. Some aspects of TA theory were checked and some major agreements about the group's work reviewed.

OUTCOMES

END OF WORKSHOP

The end of workshop feedback to the staff was very positive in terms of

1 Improved feelings and commitment towards the group and its goals
2 Greater understanding of self and others
3 Perceived increase in choices and skills in interpersonal and group behaviour.

In TA terms, the feedback reflected a general increase in Free Child (energy and creativity), Nurturing Parent (mutual support) and Adult ego-state behaviour in the group over the week, with a corresponding decrease in Critical Parent and Adapted Child behaviour. This feedback was generally endorsed by the internal course reports sent to the staff development adviser immediately after the course. In addition a number of agreements 'to do things' had been developed during the workshop which affected the group as a whole. Finally there were personal agreements to do things derived from the role negotiation activities.

ORGANISATIONAL IMPACT

The workshop produced a number of important organisational consequences, including:

Formalisation of the manager's 'role'
Some coaching and further development (training) for the manager (e.g. in such areas as leadership, decision-making and conflict management)
Support from senior management for development activities for the team generally
At least one member of the team integrating and using TA directly in his own client operations
Interest in the work from other parts of the organisation resulting in a special workshop for the internal staff development group
A feedback session with the team two months after the programme, together with some process consulting during a team meeting, i.e. on-line observation and consultation (see Chapter 15).

Feedback at two months

At one month after the workshop the team held a normal one-day meeting which was seen as being very effective and satisfactory.

At two months after the workshop, one member of the training staff attended a monthly meeting of all the team with the aims of collecting feedback from the team and observing and commenting on the performance of the team during its meeting (process consulting).

The aims of the feedback were to determine:

Felt level of self-worth and the worth of others (OK-ness)
Perceived changes in behaviour of self and others
Any resolutions of interpersonal and work problems (partly based on commitments made during workshops)
Any other comments relating to the workshop learning
Any remaining problems or problems created by the workshop.

In addition, the feedback situation in itself presented data on the general effect of the workshop on team relations and performance. The approach used was open discussion around the table, and the data is summarised in TA terms in Figure 16.13. Some general points emerge from the data:

1 It was subjective and does not represent a rigorous evaluation
2 It showed a general increase in self-confidence (OK-ness), sense of self-worth, awareness and understanding of others
3 It also showed an extensive, but not total, increase in respect for others. The group had certainly behaved discourteously to a visitor on the previous day, highlighting a problem that occurs with groups that have experienced team building programmes. This was endorsed by a new member of the team present at the feedback who saw a positive effect on team relationships and work, but intolerance to outsiders (I'm OK, you're OK, but they're not OK!)
4 Many examples were quoted, sometimes in detail, of the contribution of the workshop to resolving interpersonal difficulties and improving work effectiveness
5 There was conflicting data over the effect on family relationships
6 In general, the behaviour of the group as the feedback was given reflected what was being said in that feedback.

Figure 16.13 Some examples of the effect of the workshop from the feedback after two months, in TA terms

Decrease in 'I'm not OK' position

Increase in 'I'm OK' position (e.g. increased self-confidence)

Some decrease in 'you're not OK' position

Increase in 'you're OK' position at least as far as the team was concerned (e.g. feelings of respect and tolerance towards others)

Decrease in Critical Parent (e.g. more tolerance)

Increase in Free Child (more energy, enthusiasm for work)

Increase in Adult ('I think now instead of automatically responding')

Increased exchange of positive strokes

Decreased discounting of self and others

Increased intimacy (greater trust and openness in team)

Increased effectiveness in activity (more productive, doing more work in less time)

PROCESS CONSULTATION

As discussed in Chapter 15, TA can be used as a process consulting tool with groups who are familiar with the language and concepts. Following the feedback, the group moved ahead with its normal meeting agenda, while the workshop trainer observed and gave some feedback, using TA together with other observations. While this activity gave the group some experience of process consulting, there was a dilemma. On the one hand, there was a 'halo' effect about the staff involved in the programme and considerable value attached to their continued involvement in the development of the team. On the other hand, the team had a felt need to 'stand on its own feet'. On this basis the process consulting work was not continued.

CONCLUDING COMMENTS

This programme had as a basic feature the use of TA in a team-building activity.

The other main influence was more orthodox T-group and organisation development technology, as demonstrated by the extensive pre-course work, the concern for group-level behaviour as well as individual, the kinds of exercises used in the workshop and the language used to describe some key facets of the programme (e.g. 'trust and credibility', 'support and confrontation'). The training style used by the workshop staff was part way between the highly directive and interventionist style often used by TA trainers, and the low-profile style often adopted by T-group trainers.

The evidence is that the programme achieved its aims with distinct benefits for individual motivation and growth, team relationships, individual job performance and, less clearly, some benefits for the organisation as a whole.

It was exciting and stimulating for the staff involved as well as fruitful for the participants. The integration of TA into team building activities however needs further development and some areas emerged for further attention on another occasion. For example in the case of this programme, the issue of 'Who is the client – the organisation, the staff development adviser, the manager of the team, their (joint) boss or the team as a whole?' was discussed with the manager at length, but never fully resolved. The data from the interviews was not fed back to the team, nor did staff members attend the presentation by the manager to the team of the proposed team building workshop. A 'halo' effect developed in relation to the staff team, and in common with other approaches, the learning affected non-work relationships.

From the staff point of view, TA had established itself as a successful element in team building programmes. It also seems possible to integrate it with T-group and OD technology with positive effect.

REFERENCES

1 L.P. Bradford, J.R. Gibb and K.D. Benne, *T-Group Theory and Laboratory Method*, John Wiley, 1964.
2 R. Harrison, 'Role negotiation: A tough minded approach to team development' in *Group Training Techniques*, M.L. and P.J. Berger (eds), Gower Press, 1972.
3 T. Rickards, *Problem-Solving Through Creative Analysis*, Gower Press, 1974.

17 TA and personal growth for managers

Many of the applications discussed in this book refer to the use of TA in a highly structured manner, with the use of many exercises to support the theory inputs being made in the particular programme. Typically, the learning is very trainer-centred. The trainer retains most of the responsibility for exactly what theory inputs are made, what exercises are used and for working towards the overall goals, using an explicit programme as the vehicle.

However, it is possible to use TA in a different way for developing interpersonal skills in organisations, using a 'process group'. A process group is a group of people gathered together for a specific period of time to focus on, discuss and learn from their ongoing interactions with the others present as they occur in the 'life' of the group. In other words, participants learn from studying their own behaviour in the 'here-and-now'. In addition time may be spent focusing on how an individual's 'here-and-now' behaviour relates to behaviour in other situations, particularly work. The role of the training staff involved is to help them in this work, using whatever technology is at their disposal. As might be imagined, the relationship between participants and staff is one of the focal learning areas, particularly around the issue of authority and self-responsibility.

The aims of a process group include:

1 To gain a greater understanding of group processes and dynamics (e.g. decision-making, problem-solving, membership and leadership issues, management of work, goals, conflict and contributions, etc.)
2 To gain a greater awareness and understanding of self and relationships with others
3 To develop wider choices in terms of behaviour, i.e. not always responding in the same old stereotyped ways.

These last two aims constitute what is frequently referred to as personal growth, i.e. increase in awareness of self and others and increased choices in behaviour. A process group is not the only means for aiding personal growth but is a particularly potent one, with reasonable acceptability to organisations. The relevance of personal growth to organisations is that greater personal awareness and increased choices for interacting with others appear to be basic requirements for increased interpersonal skills (see Chapter 11).

Three well-established approaches to process groups are the T-group,[1] the Tavistock group[2] and the encounter group.[3] Over the years, various hybrids and developments have emerged from these approaches, together with the input of other technologies. One such 'technology' with an obvious and powerful input to make is TA, and the following pages examine a programme based on a mix of TA and Gestalt[4] with influences from encounter and T-group techniques. There have been some variations in the contributions from these different approaches, but the level of input from TA has stayed about the same. Others have similarly developed the use of TA in process groups using a different approach, for example Blansfield.[5] The reader may well find some difficulty in understanding the nature of the (TA-based) process group described here, unless they have experienced this approach to learning first-hand themselves. This is because this kind of learning is radically different from traditional approaches involving as it does a focus on feeling and behaving as well as thinking. This point will be referred to again later in the chapter, but suffice to say the best way to learn about process groups is to take part in one. Another consideration is that the approach is very trainee-centred, depending very much as it does on what the individual participants bring in the way of their behaviour. This variation in behaviour results in each course being significantly different in terms of learning gained.

THE AIMS OF THE COURSE

The aims of the course are:

- To increase self-awareness
- To increase learning about impact of self on others and others on self
- To increase understanding of relationships between people
- To relate this learning to the organisation situation
- To increase sense of self-worth and ability to assert (if appropriate)
- To decrease aggression and increase ability to collaborate, share with and listen to others (if appropriate)
- To increase sense of self-responsibility and ability to take responsibility for own life
- To increase range of choices in behaviour
- Where appropriate, and supported by those present, to stop dysfunctional behaviour (i.e. 'Those things I keep doing that keep landing me in trouble') and start new constructive ways of behaving.

These aims overlap considerably, and it's not possible as yet to convert them to 'tight' behavioural objectives. In this kind of training, we are in the field of personal growth and humanistic psychology with its emphasis on the unique and idiosyncratic, rather than the field of behaviourism – influenced, mechanistic, skill-based, learning courses of more orthodox training. This makes evaluation notoriously difficult (see Chapter 19).

THE COURSE PROGRAMME

The course programme, as shown in Figure 17.1, consists of a number of components – opening activities, personal diaries, large group sessions, small group counselling and closing activities. Some distinctive features of the programme are:

1 It is rather sparse compared with many programmes and is an outline only. The order of sessions often changes to deal with emerging needs
2 Normally, three staff work on the programme, but only one or two work with the group at any given time, except during the first and last sessions
3 It is impossible to say with any certainty exactly what will happen in each session, but the following sections will give some clarity.

OPENING ACTIVITIES

A number of trainer-directed opening activities and exercises are initiated and an example is shown in Figure 17.2. The inputs serve as a means of 'getting the thing off the ground' and introducing the participants to the different approach to learning. It is in the nature of the course that even the programme for these opening activities is never strictly adhered to since the activities themselves 'throw-up' important transactions between participant and participant, or between participant and staff member. As these transactions occur, staff intervene to meet the aim of developing self-awareness and all the other aims of the course.

PERSONAL DIARY

The aim of the personal diary is to structure some time each day for participants to be by themselves and focus privately on their course experiences by recording their feelings, their learning and any barriers

Figure 17.1 Programme for a 'personal growth' course for managers

9.15 a.m.	*Day 1*	*Day 2*	*Day 3*	*Day 4*	*Day 5*
		← Personal diary to 9.30 a.m. →			
		Large group	Large group	Large group	Closing activities
11.00 a.m.		Large group	Large group	Large group	Closing activities (all staff)
2.15 p.m.	Introductions (all staff)	Small group counselling	Small group counselling	Small group counselling	
4.00 p.m.	Opening activities	Large group	Large group	Large group	
7.45 p.m.	Opening activities	Large group	Large group	Large group	

Figure 17.2 Opening activity

1 Pair off with someone else in the group

2 Talk about:
   (a) Three positive personal qualities you have
   (b) Anything which you think is going to be important for that person to know to help you get the most from the course

3 We also invite you to share something about yourself (with the other person) which your immediate inclination is to hide

to learning. This focusing helps to crystallise issues for learning, and the diary also acts as a post-course record of the experience.

LARGE GROUP SESSIONS

The large group sessions are devoted to two major activities. The first is learning about self and self in relation to others, including the staff, i.e. the 'topic for discussion' is the behaviour that occurs as it occurs. As has been suggested, for those who have never experienced a process group the idea of sitting around in a circle without an apparently clear task (e.g. to discuss 'What motivates subordinates?' or 'What is the best management style?') seems strange. However, nature abhors a vacuum, silences rarely last very long and after the early uncertainty a group progressively gets to grips with the aims. The activities of the staff during this time are either individual-level interventions, using transactional analysis or Gestalt, or group-level interventions. These interventions may be extended by some exploration of the issues involved and suggestions for experimentation and change in behaviour. This point is enlarged on pp.188–189.

The other main activity of the large group sessions is theory. This may be added in small inputs during the process work, but more usually, up to two sessions (three hours) exclusively of theory are offered by the staff in any given course. If a given group opts to do theory, this is usually placed towards the end of the week. Some groups decide not to have theory, on the basis that it will interrupt the flow of the group's process and learning. Any theory sessions contributed are related to both the ongoing experiences of the week and also organisational situations. The major component is TA on the basis that it is relatively easy to transfer by individual participants to the diverse organisational backgrounds they come from. Concepts covered include: ego states, strokes, contamination and exclusion, transactions, life positions, games and time structuring. Because of the presence of the ongoing group experiences as reference material, no TA-based exercises are used.

Occasionally, structured exercises are used[6] with two aims in mind:

1 To 'energise' the group
2 To explore specific issues, e.g. leadership and membership, control and influence, listening, awareness, assertion, feedback, openness and trust, collaboration and competition, and power and authority.

SMALL GROUP COUNSELLING

These sessions involve three or four participants taking time together to reflect on their experiences, deal with more intimate issues in a 'safer' situation (most people find it easier to share personal things in small groups as opposed to large), provide mutual counselling and build up support. The staff offer their input if requested and offer guidelines for the effective use of time in these sessions. For example, participants are cautioned against involvement in the games of 'Why don't you . . ., Yes, but . . .' and 'Ain't it awful'. Staff also encourage the membership of the group to change round to give participants the maximum opportunity for interaction with others and to prevent the formation of dysfunctional cliques.

CLOSING ACTIVITIES

Separation is a recurrent event for everyone and certainly a continuous event in organisations. The break-up of groups is also a recurring feature in organisations, e.g. cessation of projects, structural reorganisations in the aftermath of takeovers, whole work units moving location, etc. The main work of the final session is consequently around the issue of separation and break-up, in the total group. It presents a final opportunity for people to say the things they've been stopping themselves from saying all week, finishing any unfinished business for themselves and learning about their own responses to the issue of separation.

THE ACTIVITIES OF THE STAFF

While the staff do not lead or direct in the traditional sense of the word, their interventions are of key importance to the development of the group. Furthermore, as we are dealing in the area of human relations not theoretically but in the 'heat of the moment', there are great demands on the staff, in terms of:

balancing caring for people with confronting people
their own self-awareness
working effectively together
technical skill (e.g. saying the most appropriate thing at the most appropriate time).

These demands in turn demand that the staff in this kind of operation pay continual attention to their own development, including attending relevant courses as participants themselves.

In order to illustrate the activites of the staff, examples of some typical TA-based interventions, with a short theoretical explanation, are shown in Figure 17.3. These interventions are made to help individuals and the group as a whole increase awareness and choices for behaviour. As part of the process of increasing awareness, the trainers encourage participants to give one another feedback. As part of the process of increasing choices, trainers suggest experiments in behaviour for the participants to carry out, e.g. 'Say something good to each person in the group in turn' or 'Instead of holding back, I want you to agree to say what you feel as you feel it from now on'.

The choice is left to the participants as to whether they take up these experiments or 'minicontracts' and their effectiveness is tested in the ongoing group process. As the group proceeds, they may be integrated as new choices in behaviour, changed and refined in the light of experience, or discarded if inappropriate.

To illustrate these points, a typical dialogue is shown in Figure 17.4.

OUTCOMES AND CONSEQUENCES

This type of learning leads to consequences that require some consideration. Firstly, the immediate reactions are very wide ranging, from the ecstatic and euphoric to total rejection. In a group of, say, twelve, the typical distribution is

Nine – positive about the experience (good to ecstatic)
Two – uncertain
One – rejection.

One interesting phenomenon is that those who are uncertain or respond negatively to the experience sometimes switch to a positive view after a period of months.[7] Some individuals (about one in forty) feel less good and confident about themselves, i.e. less OK than before.

Figure 17.3 Some TA-based interventions

Intervention	*Concept*
'You seem to have a rule about . . . '	Parent
'Think about your choices'	Adult
'I notice you're always agreeing with me'	(Compliant) Adapted Child
'It sounds as if you're sending two messages, one is . . . the other is . . .'	Ulterior transactions
'I see you are taking care of the group again'	Rescuer
'That's the fourth time today you have attempted to put someone down'	Persecutor
'It seems that you've set yourself up for a kick again'	Victim
'Notice how you denied that compliment he gave you'	Strokes
'Is this a typical feeling for you?'	Rackets

Figure 17.4 Example of typical dialogue

Bill: There's something I'm a little bit annoyed about.
Trainer: If you're only a little bit annoyed about it then it does not seem worth spending the group's time on it.
Bill: [softly] Well . . . er . . . I don't see who you are to say how the group should spend its time.
Trainer: Do you feel strongly about what I said?
Bill: No . . . not particularly, just a bit put off.
Trainer: Do you feel strongly about anybody in the group?
Bill: No, not really,
Trainer: Is there anyone you strongly like or dislike in the group?

Bill: No.
Trainer: Do you like yourself?
Bill: Not particularly.
Trainer: Tell me anything that you like about yourself.
Bill: Um . . . I'm very loyal to my company.
Trainer: That sounds like a good quality to have. Anything else?
Bill: . . . Nothing I can think of at the moment.
Trainer: Can anybody in the group identify any other positive qualities that Bill has got?
George: He's articulate.
Trainer: Express that directly to Bill.
George: You are articulate Bill and I think that is a positive quality.
Freda: You've got a good sense of humour, Bill.
Bill: People don't laugh at my jokes very often.
Trainer: Did you notice what you did with Freda's positive stroke?
Bill: . . . I dismissed it.
Trainer: What's going on with you? Aren't you worth a positive stroke?
Bill: I don't know. I don't know what you're getting at.
Trainer: So what are you feeling?
Bill: Confused . . . and frustrated.
Trainer: With whom?
Bill: With you.
Trainer: So what do you feel about me?
Bill: I'm finding you a real pain. All you do is ask questions all the time, and act so bloody detached!
Trainer: Is there anyone else you feel annoyed with? I suggest you take each person in turn in the group and experiment with expressing whatever resentments you may have about them.
Bill: I don't want to. I'm afraid people won't like me.
Trainer: That's a risk. [Silence]
Bill: Fred, I resent you sitting in silence for most of the time and acting as if you don't care about anybody.
Jean, I don't have any resentments towards you, I like you.
Tony, I'm sick to death of your intellectualising and trying to be so clever.
Dave [loudly], I'm fed up with seeing your Critical Parent so much. You're always telling people what to do!
John, I don't have any resentments towards you.
Freda, I don't know where I am with you. Sometimes I feel close to you and at other times I feel distant.
George, I resent the fact that on occasions you talk for long

periods of time and I find it confusing and boring.
Frank, I like having you around, you seem to be very stable and secure.
Trainer: Does anybody want to give Bill some feedback?
Frank: I appreciated what you said to me, Bill.
Tony: I feel I know you much better now. I think I understand you better.
Dave: You've given me something to think about. I still like you.
Trainer: What's going on now Bill?
Bill: I'm surprised. I'm surprised that I expressed my feelings so strongly and that I still seem to be accepted.
Trainer: I'd like you to experiment with expressing your feelings and resentments as they occur during the day and we'll see what happens. Are you willing to do that?
Bill: Yes . . . and I want to stop for coffee!

It is very important that the trainers offer post-course support for such people.

On the other hand, most participants experience a greater sense of OK-ness and self-confidence at the end of the course, essential pre-requisites for developing and improving interpersonal skills. This may lead to a variety of consequences. Some people find little support internally and in their post-course situation for consolidating their new learning and 'slipback' to old dysfunctional ways. Many find they do have the necessary support internally and externally (e.g. their managers' desire for them to be different outweighs their investment in the games the two of them used to play, etc.) and consolidate the learning. Still others find they have the internal support but not the external and respond to the external constraints by undertaking further developmental activities of a similar nature and/or changing jobs. In other words, they pro-act and take control of their own destiny as part of expressing their new found confidence and skills.

Apart from the 'transfer of learning' problems of this kind of work, another area requiring attention and research is that of evaluation. Much anecdotal feedback suggests that the course is effective in terms of its aims for many people, but clearly extensive systematic evaluation is an important step that is required.

SOME GENERAL COMMENTS

Personal awareness courses of the kind described in this chapter raise a number of challenging and contentious issues in terms of philosophy and aims, selection of participants and design.

PHILOSOPHY AND AIMS

This whole area of work exposes a considerable paradox for organisations. The practical consequences of personal growth and awareness for people in their managerial and employee roles in TA terms appear to be:

review/modification/rejection of Critical Parent and Adapted Child modes of behaviour
review and increase or decrease of Nurturing Parent behaviour, depending on preference for rescuing or persecuting
increase or decrease of Adult
increase of Free Child spontaneity, curiosity and energy.

Organisations have become increasingly complex both technologically and structurally in their search for power and wealth. This search has frequently been exploitative, maintaining or increasing alienation and reducing the sense of personal dignity of many employees. It has been supported by both Critical Parent based management styles and injunctions forbidding the expression of feelings (or even the experiencing of them in the first place).

The frequent outcome of this is impaired relationships with others and reduced work effectiveness. Yet organisations are highly interdependent networks or relationships between people, people who are increasingly reluctant to take 'put-downs' as a precondition of being employed. So the Critical Parent 'Don't show your feelings' culture is faced with the dilemma of an apparently successful philosophy for the growth of wealth and society actually acting as an inhibition of work effectiveness as well as personal growth and healthy relationships. Organisations frequently find themselves in an 'attraction–repulsion' bind about this kind of work, because improved personal awareness and interpersonal skills also frequently mean greater confidence and assertion and even confrontation of authority figures.

SELECTION FOR THE COURSE

Selection of participants for this kind of experience has been the subject of much discussion.[7] Four key points are:

the work role of the intending participants
the kind of people they are
the 'voluntariness' of attendance
pre-course information.

The work role of the intending participants

As far as the role is concerned, such a course is suitable not only for managers with wide and extensive spans of control, but also for specialists who have advising and influencing roles in relationship to others. The important point is that the participants work with, for or 'over' others, i.e. human contact is a daily ongoing part of their jobs.

The kind of people they are

Candidates for this kind of course usually fall into two categories: those participating on a developmental basis and those participating on a 'personal problem' basis. The former group comprise those who are already performing effectively in both the technical and interpersonal aspects of their jobs and hope to further develop their interpersonal skills by increasing their awareness and choices. The second group are those who are participating on the basis of some diagnosed 'deficiency' and 'causing' problems in their relationships with others. From the trainer's point of view it is important here to make no commitments that a definite behaviour change will be achieved but rather that an opportunity will be presented.

'Voluntariness' of attendance

The extent to which attendance is voluntary or obligatory is another important issue. It is not an 'either/or' situation that presents itself but rather a scale, something like the one shown in Figure 17.5. What is important is that people don't attend significantly 'against their will' i.e. with Adapted Child compliance covering up a Free Child 'no' (positions 1 and 2 on the scale, Figure 17.5).

Figure 17.5 The obligatory/voluntary scale for course attendance

7	I'm going (over my training officer and manager's dead bodies, if need be!)
6	I'm going (I even selected the course and my training officer and manager agree)
5	I wanted to do something like this, and they've found me a course that looks useful
4	They suggested a course might help and I agree
3	They suggested this course and I don't mind too much
2	I don't want to go, but I suppose I'd better
1	I don't want to go!

Pre-course information

For most management training courses, participants can at least safely predict the learning process (lectures, discussions, use of video, role plays, exercises, etc.) if not the learning content. The problem here is that even the learning process (focusing on here-and-now behaviour, and feeling and doing as well as thinking) is very alien to many after a lifetime of experiencing more traditional educational and training approaches. To prepare people for the experience of the course discussed in this chapter, pre-course notes are sent out and backed up by telephone discussions.

The pre-course notes cover:

- the aims of the course
- the methods of the course
- the role of the staff
- the nature of the experience and optimum ways to gain from it.

Of course, pre-course notes themselves are a cognitive device, but at least people get the message that this is something different! Discussions are held with participants with the aims of:

- determining whether the attendance is developmental or problem based
- determining the extent to which participation is voluntary or obligatory
- determining the support for the course from the individual's manager (e.g. has the individual discussed the pre-course notes with his boss?)
- determining the understanding by the individual of the nature and aims of the experience
- giving either the individual an opportunity to withdraw from the programme or the staff member an opportunity to advise withdrawal.

DESIGN AND OPERATION

The operation of a course of this kind raises a number of considerations.

Boundary between training and therapy

This issue is at its most acute in personal awareness and growth type courses, and is discussed more fully in Chapter 19. Suffice to say that the trainer has to be clear in his own mind about the boundary.

Behaviour of the trainer(s) in ego-state terms

As described in a previous section, personal awareness and growth courses are in themselves very confronting and ambiguous situations for many. People are asked to do such things as:

sit in a circle, with no desks to hide behind
talk to one another about their behaviour as it happens
share their feelings as well as their thoughts
accept a leadership style lower in direction than that to which they are usually accustomed
operate with a relatively low future certainty (see the programme, Figure 17.1)
operate in a situation where there are sometimes silences, and often events are deliberately slowed down.

These characteristics of the situation are likely to lead to escalation of Adapted Child responses. At this point, it is important for the staff to work from an OK position, using Nurturing Parent and Adult to maximise the learning from the 'here-and-now' and to provide a solid basis for trust to develop through the week's activities. Correspondingly, the use of positive Critical Parent can be increased during the week. The three 'P's' (protection, permission and potency) as used by TA therapists offer useful guidelines to the style of the trainer in this situation, though in modified form.[8] For the development of awareness (through the readiness to receive feedback) and choices (through personal experimentation) participants need to experience protection from the trainer's Parent (i.e. 'This is a safe place to be'), permission again from the trainer's Parent (i.e. 'This is a place to explore and make changes') and potency from the trainer's Free Child (i.e. the trainers are powerful enough to help the participant to over-rule dysfunctional messages influencing his or her life).

Group process and integration

In the kind of course described in this chapter, the group are working and living together over five days and consequently the total dynamic of the group needs attention. Now, TA (and Gestalt) are trainer-centred individually-orientated approaches, with the group as a kind of support rather than an entity on its own. There is a risk as a consequence that the group develops an over-dependence on the trainer. The group consequently ends up treating the trainer as an omnipotent expert rather than a resource, hence actually interfering in the autonomy and self-responsibility aim of TA. Attention to the process of group development, and intervening appropriately, help to manage this issue. Clearly the integration of individually-orientated approaches (TA and Gestalt) with group-orientated (T-group and Tavistock group) requires future investigation.

REFERENCES

1 L.P. Bradford, J.R. Gibb and K.D. Benne, *T-Group Theory and Laboratory Method*, John Wiley, 1964.
2 W.R. Bion, *Experiences in Groups*, Tavistock Publications, 1961.
3 A. Burton (ed), *Encounter; The Theory and Practice of Encounter Groups*, Jossey Bass Inc., 1970.
4 S.M. Herman and M. Korenich, *Authentic Management: A Gestalt Orientation to Organisations and their Development*, Addison-Wesley, 1977.
5 M.G. Blansfield, 'Transactional analysis as a training intervention' in *Modern Theory and Method in Group Training*, W.G. Dyer (ed), Litton Educational Publishing Inc., 1972.
6 J.W. Pfeiffer and J.E. Jones, *A Handbook of Structured Experiences for Human Relations Training*, vols 1 to 6, University Associates, 1969 onwards.
7 C.L. Cooper and D. Bowles, 'Hurt or helped', *Training Information Paper* no. 10, Training Services Agency, 1977.
8 C.M. Steiner, *Scripts People Live*, Grove Press Inc., 1974; Bantam Books, 1975.

18 Other areas of application

Chapters 12 to 17 give some detailed thoughts and reports on the application of TA in organisations. One of the strengths of TA is its wide range of potential uses in organisations, and in this chapter three more areas of use are briefly dealt with: TA in customer and public contact (particularly in selling), TA for senior secretaries, and TA in 'middle-escence'. The chapter concludes with a wide, but not all-embracing, summary of areas of application of TA.

TA FOR CUSTOMER AND PUBLIC CONTACT

One of the commonest areas of application for TA in organisations has been customer and public contact training, and the work with in-flight staff and booking clerks at American Airlines (the TACT programme) was one of the first major industrial TA training programmes carried out.[1] The aim of TA in these situations has been generally to aid 'smoother', more comfortable interaction in a situation where the contact is often transitory. This is particularly the case in the context of public contact, e.g. bank clerks, post office clerks, booking clerks, etc., where the TA input can be largely restricted to ego states, transactions, strokes and stamps, supported with audio-visual aids. In some kinds of selling e.g. long-term sale, installation and service of high-cost capital goods, the more extensive relationship developed with the client may lead to games and this would then be an important input into any training given.

The use of TA in these situations often raises the question: 'For whose comfort is the TA training done, the trainee or the customer?' Behind this is the more fundamental issue of to what extent is TA training of this kind supporting manipulation because of the involvement of a financial transaction (purchase of goods or services) with interpersonal transactions. This depends on the extent to which the customer is a passive thing to be exploited by the salesman, with no influence on the decision-making process involved and no responsibility for what happens. TA would suggest that the customer is ultimately responsible for his or her own behaviour, though this is not to deny the existence of 'sharp practices', nor to condone the use of TA to support such practices.

The next section looks specifically at the use of TA in selling.

TA IN SELLING

The first important point to make is that TA can be used as a powerful tool in conjunction with established selling skills, but in no way replaces those skills. Most salesmen are trained to view the selling process as a series of identifiable steps leading to the customer placing the order. A large number of selling systems of varying complexity have developed over the years, some involving seven or eight steps, some just a beginning, middle and end. During training each of those steps is accompanied by 'dos and don'ts', and TA often endorses the wisdom of these 'rules'. Sometimes, however, it does suggest some reconsideration.

It is generally recognised that many sales are won or lost before the salesman actually meets the customer, even if what the salesman has to sell meets a clear and demonstrable need of the client's. The reasons for this are varied. A typical example is any unfinished business carried around by potential customers from previous transactions with other parties; salesmen can be convenient external figures to dump brown stamps on.

Now, by using TA as a model to look at the opening contact between salesman and customer, and by analysing the potential situation beforehand, it may be possible to reduce the incidence of sales lost prior to the contact.

Consider a salesman entering the premises of a new customer for the first time. In this potentially uncertain situation – new client, new organisation – there is a risk of slipping into Adapted Child behaviour, e.g. being subservient, deferential, unassertive, or defensive. The risk is that this behaviour is probably going to activate the customer's Critical Parent, as in Figure 18.1. Thus any not-OK Adapted Child behaviour is likely to reduce the chances of getting a sale right at the beginning. (This is not to rule out the use of normal Adapted Child rituals, such as 'Good Morning, how are you?') This is likely to be exacerbated by any contaminations carried by the customer, e.g.

> 'Salesmen can't be trusted.'
> 'All salesmen are out to catch the customers.'
> 'They're only interested in meeting their forecasts, not our needs.'

Of course, the contaminations are true for a few salesmen. On the other hand, a customer operating from his Adult without these contaminations knows that salesmen sell things to people who need them, and as long as he stays in his Adult there are no strings attached and he has the right to say no.

There are a few salesmen who are adept at hooking the Nurturing

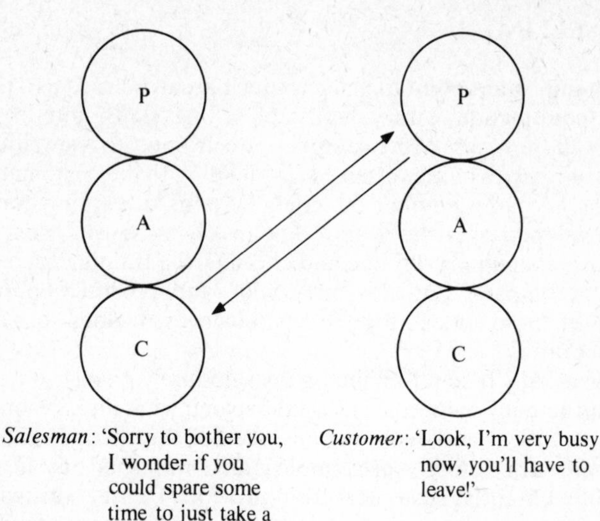

Figure 18.1 Salesman in Adapted Child – Customer in Critical Parent

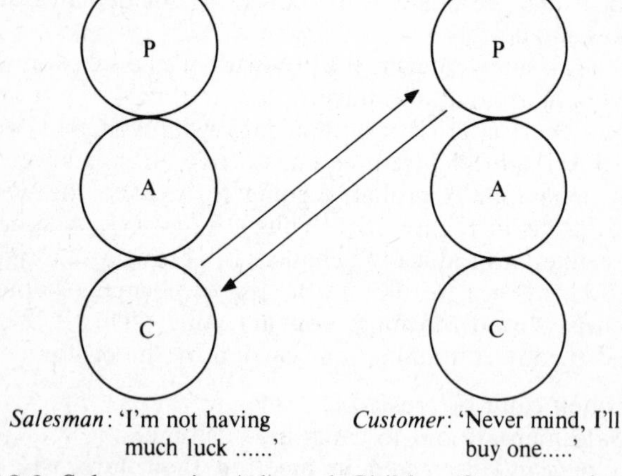

Figure 18.2 Salesman in Adapted Child – Customer in Nurturing Parent

Parent in customers and some customers who often respond to this, so that the salesman gets his orders by people taking care of him, as in Figure 18.2.

Perhaps the worst opening for a salesman to make is from the Critical Parent, particularly if the client responds similarly as in Figure 18.3. In most situations, the best opening is likely to be from the Adult,

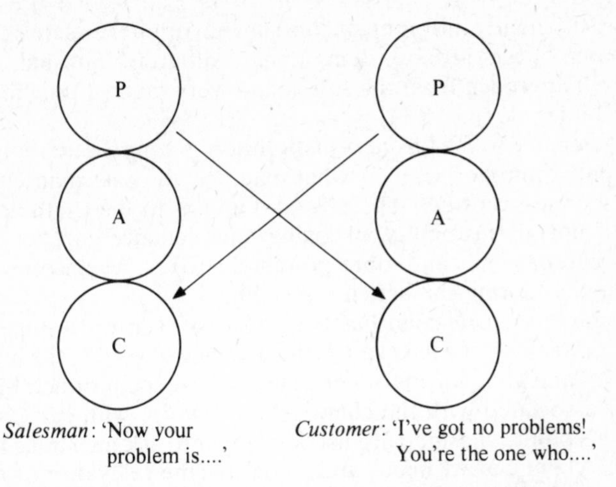

Figure 18.3 Salesman and customer both in Critical Parent

based on a position of mutual respect in relation to the customer (I+ U+).

Very often the salesman will have some prior knowledge and experience of the customer and will be able to use this to determine the most appropriate behaviour and transactions for opening the sale. However, a word of caution: not everyone is predictable and the problem with 'rehearsing a line' is that the customer is not always in the anticipated ego state that the opening transactions were designed for. This is where the Little Professor may well be useful in intuitively sensing the 'mood' of the potential customer. After all, one of the important things about having a plan is to be prepared to change it.

Every salesman has been taught the importance of getting the client's attention in order to move on to productive communication. So far the importance of:

the Adult – for listening
the Little Professor – for sensing 'where the client is'
the positive Adapted Child – for politeness and expected social conventions

has been discussed. To this might be added:

the Nurturing Parent – for showing concern in relation to the client's needs (though with discretion).

The Free Child is important too. In order to gain attention, the salesman and his/her product have to be 'different' in some way from every other salesman and product the client is going to see. The product itself may be sufficiently different and unique, but often there are some very good competitors around, demanding a different, unusual, creative and fresh approach from the salesman – very much a function of the Free Child.

Another side to the business of attention-getting is attention-giving, or to put it another way, to what extent is the salesman customer-centred or self-centred? There is no doubt as to the usefulness, with some if not all customers, of giving 'maintenance' strokes through rituals and pastimes and more powerful strokes, where relevant and not phoney, during the activity of selling.

Assuming the salesman has been successful in capturing the customer's attention, the next step is the dual one of getting the interest of the client and arousing his or her desire to have the product. Interest is mainly associated with the client's Adult, desire with the Child.

At this point, salesmen are usually taught to ask questions to ascertain the client's exact needs and so ensure the relevance of the sale. However, there are two important points to remember and pay attention to at this stage. First, legitimate questions from the Adult will further the selling process. Phoney questions from the Little Professor to set others up or hostile questions from the Critical Parent to put them down will get in the way. An awareness of questioning style is therefore of particular assistance to the salesman. Second, too many questions can lead to an 'overkill' situation hooking the customer's Critical Parent or rebellious part of the Adapted Child. Alternatively, continued use of logical Adult-based discussion and questioning may end up boring the customer's Child and switching him off.

Techniques used for creating desire are worth examining. One choice is the angular ulterior transaction (see Chapter 4) using such apparent Adult–Adult transactions to hook the customer's Child as:

> 'It's the last one I've got.'
> 'It's very expensive.'
> 'Of course some old-fashioned companies won't buy this product.'

Salesmen are notorious for the use of this particular, manipulative style. Another choice is to relate to the Free Child of the customer with genuine enthusiasm, fun and humour, i.e. with the salesman's own Free Child, backed up by straight talking from the Adult. This avoids the risk with the angular transaction of leaving a sense of 'being conned' and hence resentment.

A sizeable issue in sales training is how to deal with objections from the customer. After all, few sales calls are without the raising of some objections. TA raises some useful points here:

1 Some objections are legitimate, based on the customer's Adult appraisal of the situation
2 Some objections originate from the customer's Critical Parent or (rebellious) Adapted Child
3 It is important for a salesman to use his or her feelings and process in relation to the customer to identify which ego state is the source of the objection. This is because of the risk of being drawn into games by the customer's Critical Parent or Adapted Child and thus increasing the risk of losing the sale and ending up with bad feelings (frustration, anger, inadequacy, disappointment, humiliation, etc.)
4 As a consequence, the best way of dealing with objections is to stay firmly in the Adult.

The closing stage of a sale is when the salesman asks for the order and the client responds appropriately. Effective closing is certainly the point at which many successful salesmen can be identified and sometimes failure here is a consequence of the salesman hesitating to ask for the order. Failure to ask directly or positively suggests over-adapted behaviour and consequently runs the risk once more of hooking a Critical Parent response.

The salesman needs to use his Adult ego state, perhaps with Free Child, at this point. The question of how to ask for the order raises the big question 'From which ego state does a person make the decision to buy?' It is questionable whether people make buying decisions solely in a rational logical way. For many people, the other ego states are often involved and indeed may 'override' the Adult, even if the product is highly technical and/or expensive (see Figure 18.4).

Figure 18.4 Decisions to buy based on customer ego states other than the Adult

Nurturing Parent	'You've had a rough time recently, you need to spoil (stroke) yourself'
Free Child	'Heh! It would be fun to have one of those'
Adapted Child (hooked by an angular transaction)	'I'm not as poor as you think' 'I'll show you I can afford it'

THE USE OF TA IN A COURSE FOR SENIOR SECRETARIES

THE SETTING AND THE NEED

This course involved as participants some senior secretaries working for a large organisation. They had been with their employer for a long time and reached the top in their careers as secretaries, all of them working for senior managers in the organisation.

The need for the course was based on three main concerns. First, there had been some major administrative changes which the organisation wished to bring to the attention of the senior secretaries and discuss with them the effects of these changes. Second, a number of circumstances had emphasised the need for training secretaries in communication skills. This reflected a growing realisation that, although the secretary does not hold a position of formal responsibility, her job as an agent of communication and her relationship with her boss, and his colleagues and subordinates, could have a big impact on the effectiveness of the organisation. Third, some secretaries had gained a vicarious power by proxy from their bosses, giving them a distorted view of their role.

THE AIMS OF THE COURSE

The course was designed to:

1 Present and discuss new administrative changes
2 Help the secretaries gain further insight into their role particularly in terms of communications
3 Help them appreciate more fully the problem areas of their work
4 Give them an opportunity to develop their abilities and choices, and formulate a personal life plan.

Considerable attention was paid to developing a supportive and nurturing climate during this work, particularly to support the last of the aims.

THE COURSE CONTENT

The course involved twelve participants and two trainers and was spread over two days. TA was introduced on the second day and included:

1 Ego states and transactions, supported by exercises (particular attention was devoted to managing Critical Parent and

Adapted Child behaviour in others)
2 Life positions, including an opportunity for the secretaries to recognise their own favourite position in the OK corral
3 The drama triangle, with the drama triangle exercise (Chapter 16).

The final half-day of the course was devoted to a life-planning activity based on three questions:

'Where am I now?' (an assessment of career and personal development to date)
'Where do I want to be?' (producing ideas about the future)
'How do I get there?' (making realistic plans and generating agreements with other course members to carry out those plans)

These three questions were elaborated in the form of a questionnaire completed by each participant. The questionnaire used such concepts as ego states, life positions and the drama triangle, already introduced to the participants.

The questionnaire stage was followed by small group counselling supervised by the trainers. When appropriate some basic ideas from script theory (e.g. injunctions, permissions) were introduced into the small groups.

OUTCOMES

One month after the course, participants expressed their appreciation of the introduction to TA, confirmed they had found numerous applications for it and recommended that others be given an opportunity to attend the course. As a consequence, a series of similar courses has been planned for other senior secretaries.

TA AND 'MIDDLE-ESCENCE'

The previous section described a programme where some aspects of scripts were introduced as an aid to developing life planning for women (senior secretaries). An intriguing and important development of the application of scripts to men in organisations has come through the work of Novey,[2] using TA in conjunction with the idea of 'middle-escence', sometimes referred to as the 'mid-life' crisis. Mid-life crisis in men has been the subject of some attention recently[3] and Novey presents a TA-based model for looking at this phenomenon and dealing with it.

Many organisations face problems with those middle-aged managers who were once highly considered, but have now lost their motivation, interest, commitment and productivity. This group (referred to by Novey as 'deadwood') confront the organisation to achieve a balance between effectiveness and caring.

Deadwood often have what are referred to as 'almost winner' scripts (Figure 18.5). This kind of script is based on conditional stroking for achievement, rather than closeness to others. In other words, in adulthood men with this script get high internal strokes from their influencing Parent ego state for achievement (but often low positive external stroking for successful work!). However, despite their scripting 'almost winners' frequently switch to a losing streak, usually during their forties. Two external factors are relevant here. First, achievement demands time and energy, but the opportunities for promotion decrease with the increase in level of status, so the competition gets fiercer. Second, many men find by the time they are forty that they are fairly stable economically (e.g. the mortgage is nearly paid off) and their children are becoming independent. With the pressures of income and children declining, some take the time to think: 'How did I get here? 'What's it all about?' 'Was all the competition worth it?' 'Why is it so difficult to get close to people?'

Figure 18.5 'Almost winner' script

I am usually OK and usually approve of myself
I can almost win (succeed)
Don't be better than . . .
Be cautious about feelings
Work first, fun later (maybe)
Give and get some strokes, but not too many
Run your own life with the following limits . . .
Be cautious about others

This signals the onset of middle-escence. Chapter 2 described a TA view of early development.[4] Any unresolved issues from that time are recycled and worked on again during adolescence (for example, the ages 16 to 18 are characterised by considerable arguing about Parent values, just as at 7 to 10). The same kind of developmental issues are recycled for a second time, usually starting sometime between 35 and 45. At this point, as shown in Figure 18.6, if those with 'non-winner' scripts do not work through these issues satisfactorily, they may well become deadwood, i.e. if the middle-escence issues are not resolved, they get in the way of energy, creativity and motivation.

The response of organisations to 'deadwood' is varied: get rid of,

Figure 18.6 Middle-escence issues (starting at 40 years)

Actual age	*Developmental age*	*Issues*
40	1	Feeding and stroking (e.g. tastes, fitness)
45	2	Symbiosis with spouse and organisation. Feel tied down, restrained, frustrated. How to be independent, get strokes from others, and yet not feel tied by stroke suppliers?
50	3 to 6	Script rewriting
55	7 to 10	Parent values Religious and philosophical issues

kick upstairs, early retirement, shunt sideways. Unfortunately, there is often a cost to organisations, through the loss of a large investment in time and money in the individual, by virtue of his inefficiency while thinking what to do with him and frequently by the effect on the morale of others.

However, there is another choice, which is for the organisation to grasp the initiative. Novey suggests it is possible to run workshops for managers to resolve middle-escence problems. These use script theory to discover early injunctions and TA generally to change destructive adapted behaviours. There are two problems to be resolved in doing this however. First, working with organisational groups is not the same as working with therapy groups. Novey suggests the use of small discussion groups, for example, as an aid to providing the right balance of support and confrontation, without creating too much anxiety and scare. A second point to be considered is that organisations, like families, often have a vested interest in people not changing, so that 'in organisational work a large part of the effort needs to be applied to changing the organisational environment, particularly along the lines of stroking levels and protection available'.

SUMMARY OF THE APPLICATIONS OF TA

To summarise the potential uses of TA in organisations it is convenient to divide the activities of organisations into those at the 'boundary', involving contact with external parties, and those to do solely with internal relationships.

BOUNDARY RELATIONSHIPS

Selling, customer and *public contact, advising, consulting* and other activities to do with the main goals of the organisation are highly relevant areas for the application of TA. This applies whatever the goals of the organisation, e.g. manufacturing, distribution, providing a service, monitoring standards in relation to government legislation, etc. TA may also be helpful in the *recruitment process* and in the *induction* of new employees. One possible area of use is in negotiating with other external parties, e.g. commercial and trade union negotiations. Use of TA for manager–union negotiations raises particular problems. Trade unions are often very suspicious of the behavioural sciences, and operate with a collectivist philosophy apparently dissonant with the individualist philosophy of TA. TA may still be a help, though, to a management team in negotiations.

INTERNAL RELATIONSHIPS

Within an organisation, TA can be used for generally improving communication and interpersonal relationships. More specifically TA can contribute to developing the *leadership* function through examining *management style*. The *training of trainers* is a particular application where TA has significant benefits in helping professional trainers in their group leading skills. As far as *groups* are concerned TA can contribute generally to *group membership* skills. (In organisational psychology much is talked about leadership skills, but little about membership!) It is clearly relevant to *problem-solving* and *decision-making* processes in groups and may prove to be a very useful adjunct to developing *creativity*, using the concept of the Free Child.

Its most potent application at the group level is probably *team building*. Many problems in organisations are caused by the conflict between groups, and TA may well be of value to *inter-group communication and negotiation*. TA has already been of use in helping cultural minority groups and women in asserting themselves and developing their sense of 'OK-ness' in organisations.[1]

TA has established itself as a powerful technique in developing *interpersonal relationships*, to help people with *influencing* skills, *assertion* and handling *authority* issues in constructive ways. It has general application to all kinds of two-person situations in organisations, including *interviewing*, *peformance appraisal*,[5] *coaching* and *counsel-*

ling. It is of considerable value to people in developing their *personal awareness* and *self-motivation*. One additional and as yet largely unexplored area, is *career development* and the process of developing life plans and goals.

Finally TA can be used as an integral part of a total *organisation development* and *change* effort, including such areas as *job enrichment* (e.g. using the concept of strokes) and *participation* (see Chapter 15).

REFERENCES

1 D. Jongeward et al., *Everybody Wins: TA Applied to Organisations*, Addison-Wesley, 1973.
2 T.B. Novey, *TA for Management*, Jalmar Press Inc., 1976.
3 C.F. Molander, 'Management development and the middle aged manager', *Personnel Review*, vol. 6, no. 2, 1977.
4 P. Levin, *Becoming the Way we Are. A Transactional Guide to Personal Development*, Group House, Berkeley, 1974.
5 J.H. Morrison and J.J. O'Hearne, *Practical Transactional Analysis in Management*, Addison-Wesley, 1977.

19 Evaluation, limitations and benefits

EVALUATION

Transactional analysis is now at the stage where a substantial evaluation[1,2] of its effects in organisations is required. It is being sufficiently widely used for the consequences of its use and the accuracy of its claims to need checking. More specifically:

1 Is it improving the personal awareness and/or social skills of those exposed to it?
2 How does it compare with other approaches to interpersonal skills training? Does it have any advantages or limitations in comparison with them?
3 What is its impact on the organisation as a whole?
4 What are the risks or disadvantages associated with its use?[3]
5 How can we improve its use?

Compared with evaluating the effectiveness of manual skill training, evaluating interpersonal skills training is not an easy task. The nature of the learning is often so very divergent – different people learn different things. How would you 'measure' authenticity, intimacy and spontaneity? The 'ultimate' aims of TA may well transcend the restrictions of classical scientific thinking. In any case, do people need scientists to prove their statement that they feel better about themselves and others?

One feature of TA may well be very helpful in its evaluation. TA embodies a series of concepts associated with discrete observable behaviour categories. With sufficient planning and resources it should be possible to observe participants before and after TA training, and measure the changes in these categories, e.g. stroking patterns. This is going to be easier with situations internal to the organisation (e.g. a working team) than with those involving contact with external parties (customers, etc.).

Currently, the measurement of the effectiveness and consequences of TA is individual and anecdotal. A typical example is the feedback from the team building programme (Chapter 16). However, some attempts have been made at a more systematic follow up. One notable example was the TACT (TA for Customer Treatment) programme carried out in 1971.[4]

In 1971, American Airlines were experiencing a decrease in customer ratings. Their response was to put over 6,000 employees (ground and in-flight staff) in seven months through a TA programme. Some of the key features of the programme were:

ego states, transactions and games as the major concepts used
tape/slide presentation and discussion as the approach to learning
line managers and supervisors were trained as trainers
four to eight participants were present in each training group.

Evaluation by questionnaire of 600 participants was carried out two to three months after the programme of training. The data was generally encouraging. For example,

58% said, 'I feel I'm doing my job more efficiently'
78% said, 'I am somewhat/much more positive about job'
66% said, 'I now see myself somewhat/very differently from what I did before'
65% said, 'Since TACT programme customers receive better/much better treatment'

However,

26% of supervisors did not hold post-programme discussions with participants, and most important of all, the courtesy ratings stayed the same or continued to decline.

While the questionnaire data was generally positive and backed up by much positive anecdotal material, the programme failed to have an impact on the problem it was designed to resolve. The author, Lyman Randall, postulated two reasons for this:

1 Individual learning is not enough. Brief training programmes with minimal follow-up will probably not cause major or lasting organisational change; a fact well known to organisation development specialists
2 Individual learning which is not reinforced will probably not be applied. Even though two or three levels of management above the customer service employee received TACT training, the managers apparently did little to reinforce TA applications.

Nevertheless, the author concludes, the potential application of TA to large-scale organisation change strategies still appears both promising and exciting.

PROBLEMS AND LIMITATIONS

TA is certainly not a perfect answer to all human relationships problems in organisations, families or society as a whole. It does have problems and limitations, some theoretical and philosophical, some very practical, and these will be considered in this chapter.

THEORETICAL BASIS

The theoretical basis of TA has been subject to criticism from at least one source.[5] TA may indeed fall short of the demands of classical scientific logic, being more a hypothesis or model than a theory. This is generally true of the other recent and related developments in humanistic psychology. The whole development of the natural sciences in the twentieth century has been in the context of increasing awareness of the limitations of the assumptions on which scientific thought and philosophy is itself based[6] – a fact frequently ignored by sociologists and psychologists in their attempt to emulate the rigorous thinking of the natural sciences in their exploration of human behaviour (see Chapter 10).

TA then, does not stand up to precise scientific examination. Further, it is an analytical model, based on the categorisation of behaviours, and an interpretative model, with special meanings being ascribed to those behaviours. Inevitably, this use of labelling results in some loss of meaning as well as some gain. In attempting to analyse the 'moving target' of human behaviour and experience, some things are inevitably left out or missed, and consequently, like all analytical approaches, it does not provide a total description and interpretation of the human condition.

Perhaps the important issue is a much more practical one. If we look at TA as a model, can we use it, and if we do, does it in some way increase our sense of well-being, confidence, happiness, ability to relate to others and work with them effectively, or whatever other indicators we may use to signify an improvement in the condition of people? Currently, the answer is yes, albeit on the basis of fragmentary, and non-rigorous, often anecdotal and individual evidence.

THE POTENCY OF TA

TA is a potent method, but not omnipotent. One of the current problems is its indiscriminate use as a panacea, the 'ultimate' in human relationships training in industry. It may be inevitable that there is a 'band-wagon' effect – as is often true for new approaches. It seems likely that as it becomes more established and as both its usefulness and its limitations become clearer, there will be a levelling off in its application.

THE CULTURAL ORIGINS

TA, like much of humanistic psychology, originated in white middle-class America and bears characteristics of that particular cultural milieu, e.g. its stress on individual responsibility. In other ways, it runs counter to that culture, e.g. in its value of caring, collaborative and authentic relationships as opposed to the manipulative and competitive ones endemic in some parts of Western society. Its individualistic ethos certainly brings it into conflict with the collectivism of Marxism. Its origins may therefore be a barrier to its usefulness in dealing with social change issues related to iniquitous distributions of wealth and power and also its acceptability in cultures with strong collective influences. On the other hand, some aspects are very helpful in this area. Its basic ideas are fairly easily understood even by the less educated and/or less intelligent, it does seem to offer particular help to those who give power away in their relationships, and it has been applied with some success in developing the skills and well-being of some dispossessed groups.

LANGUAGE OF TA

The objective of developing a language that is easily shared has led to some problems. First, a tendency for the words to be used in a casual way, without any real insight or understanding. Second, risks of rejection of TA because of its language as opposed to its ideas and methodology. For example, in using TA in British organisations, trainers are sometimes faced with a general rejection of this latest gimmick from the US (primarily from a contamination, but not without foundation since British managers have been inundated with 'ultimate models' of organisational and personal behaviour over the last two decades mainly stemming from the other side of the Atlantic) and, more specifically, with acceptance of the basic model but unhappiness and discomfort with the labels used. There certainly does not seem to be any reason why words cannot be changed to fit the cultural situation, *provided the original meaning of the concept is not lost.*

MANIPULATION

There is no doubt that TA can be used, by those who so desire, to put other people down and otherwise manipulate them, though this is a problem shared by other approaches to interpersonal skills training.

To some extent the message is in the method itself, i.e. the exposure of manipulative strategies and the value laid on authentic contact. Trainers can also help to reduce the likelihood of manipulation by the example of their own behaviour (this in turn demands that trainers should constantly look at and work on their own process). This will help to the extent that at least some participants will look for congruence between a trainer's behaviour and his material and will model by identification accordingly. Trainers can also caution trainees against using TA manipulatively.

Whatever steps are taken, there are still likely to be occasions when people leave training courses where TA has been used as a component, and use it to manipulate or put others down. As Groder has pointed out[7] psycho- and sociopathic personalities will abuse anything for their own ends, and for these people (yes, there are some in organisations) a greater range and depth of intervention is required.

As a whole TA practitioners value the development of collaborative, not competitive, relationships (just as T-group trainers do), together with assertion, but not manipulation or aggresion. The general experience is that TA helps people to gain more power over their own lives rather than over the lives of others. Also TA, together with other similar approaches, may raise issues for those who have an investment in someone *not* changing their behaviour. For example a boss may be threatened by a subordinate changing his or her traditional victim mode of behaviour, as it threatens his dominant persecutor position in their transactions. At the individual level, the answer to this is to provide adequate pre- and post-training support, and perhaps ultimately to consider using TA in a whole department or organisation.

I'M OK, YOU'RE NOT OK

In common with other approaches TA has the challenge of dealing directly with people whose basic life position is I+ U−. Whereas TA therapists deal with individuals who by and large feel 'not OK' in some sense, trainers frequently deal with those who feel 'I'm OK, you're not OK'. This is because (in Britain at least) TA is not an establishment choice in therapy and the majority of clients on TA therapy workshops are self-nominated, paying for themselves. However clients on training courses are sent and paid for by their nominating organisation. Trainers often encounter aggression and hostility from participants in an I+ U− position who see no reason to examine their relationships and make changes ('It's everybody else's fault' or 'It's everybody else who's no good, inadequate', etc.).

Such people sometimes come to reject TA. Again, the nature of our organisational cultures is such that the norms of competition and manipulation lead to those with dominant I+ U− often 'getting to the top'. In this position their response to all forms of training is all too frequently 'We don't need it (because we've made it) but "that lot" (middle and junior managers) do'. If in turn 'that lot' start to assert themselves, the top in turn, in the absence of adequate consultation and education by the TA trainer, may reject any further work.

TRAINING AND QUALIFICATIONS

TA theory is now very extensive, demands time to digest and even more time to develop skills in its use, certainly more time than some other approaches to analysing behaviour. Anyone using TA in a substantial way is strongly advised to develop their professional skills and personal self-knowledge continually through appropriate courses, workshops and extensive reading. Using TA after reading a few books is totally inadequate because of the potency of TA. At the other extreme, the enforcement of qualifications as a pre-requisite to using the approach carries serious risks of developing sterility and rigidity of thought and application, and also the risk of developing 'professional imperialism' and exclusivity, which is contrary to a basic value of Berne's.

MISCONCEPTIONS

Some misconceptions about TA values and beliefs exist. A notable one is that TA professionals and followers value the use of the Adult ego state above all else and the Critical Parent and Adapted Child are somehow not respectable. The actual value is that people should be able to use any ego state according to the needs of the situation.

TRAINING AND THERAPY

The fact that TA originated as an approach to psychotherapy has certainly been seen by some as sufficient reason to reject its possible use in organisations. However, there is a view that all effective approaches to training, education, counselling, therapy and rehabilitation have a common basis at least in terms of developing people in all their various capacities.[8,9] The boundary between training and therapy is nevertheless an important one, and trainers need to be clear in this respect. At a practical level, there are some techniques that are clearly not appropriate for trainers, e.g. prompting people to re-experience archaic family issues. Some theory areas need to be introduced with discretion, particularly scripts. Another contentious issue, not unique to TA, is the extent to which TA encourages 'acting out' and release and expression of feelings such as anger, grief and joy, with physical contact. Physical contact, other than the usual ritualised forms, between managers on a training course is usually considered taboo. Also any human relations type training runs the risk of participants getting in touch with long submerged memories and emotions, and the possibility, for example, of someone crying. This last situation frequently gets exaggerated on the organisational grapevine to: 'Did you hear, Jim Smith had a nervous breakdown on that course he went to last week, isn't that awful!' It is certainly true that the development of the T-group raised concerns in some psychiatric circles and it is likely that any new approach to interpersonal skills training will do the same.

At a philosophical level, it seems most appropriate that trainers operate with an educational or developmental model of human beings (i.e. someone who already has interpersonal skills that can be broadened) rather than a 'medical' or therapy model (i.e. 'man, the sick animal').

ADVANTAGES AND BENEFITS

TA has a number of advantages and benefits in its use which are fundamental to its current growth of application. Some of these are shared by other approaches, some are specific to TA.

CLARITY

It is a relatively clear and concise model of human behaviour (compared with, say, psychoanalysis). Its use of short appealing words and phrases as opposed to elaborate technical ones help it to be readily understood by large numbers of people of different backgrounds and levels of intelligence and education, even very young children.

FACE-VALIDITY AND ACCEPTABILITY

The particular words and phrases help it have a high face-validity. Many people readily identify with the concepts and can easily relate them to their own experiences of themselves and others. It consequently has a high degree of acceptability.

COMMON LANGUAGE

Because of the language used, it offers a concise and common way for a group of people, including an organisation, to describe their behavioural transactions. This is parallel to an organisation having a common financial language for monetary transactions.

LINKED THEORY OF PERSONALITY, COMMUNICATION AND DESTINY

The theory of communications element is probably the most important for organisational use. It is not just theory of communication (transactions and games) though. It is also a theory of personality (ego states) and destiny (time structuring and scripts) – both important dimensions for organisations.

It may also provide a model for examining the effects of the organisational demands of role, structure, systems and procedures on individual behaviour and interpersonal communication, though this area has hardly been explored.

INTEGRATED THEORY OF THINKING, FEELING AND BEHAVING

It deals with thinking, feeling, and verbal and non-verbal modes of behaving. This gives particular power to TA if one agrees with Kurt Lewin, a key figure in the development of group dynamics and T-groups.[8] His view was that effective personal change, whether through training, counselling, therapy or rehabilitation, required changing at all these levels (thinking, feeling and behaving). This seems to give TA some advantages over some other approaches to interpersonal skill training, for example T-groups which operate at the feeling and behaving level and behaviour analysis[2] which operates at the behaviour level only. TA is not necessarily dissonant with these approaches however, and can clearly be integrated with T-group technology, as shown in Chapter 17. Very often T-group trainers and TA facilitators are talking about the same thing but using different words (T-groups – 'support', TA – 'protection', T-groups – 'trust and openness', TA – 'intimacy'). It seems likely that integration with other approaches will be a major future developmental activity for TA.

FLEXIBILITY

As a training method, it is capable of 'fine-tuning', i.e. the nature of the input can be varied depending on the time available, the knowledge, experience and attitudes of the learning group, and the nature of the relationship between the trainer, the learning group and the employing organisation(s). This flexibility is elaborated in Chapter 11.

RETENTION

Because of the theory of personality and individual behaviour at its core the retention of learning does not appear to be so dependent on the dynamics and cohesion of the learning group compared with some other approaches. Many people find that after a suitable learning programme they can continue to use and apply TA in examining their relationships, giving them wider and more effective choices in varying situations, even though there may be no support from the organisation.

TRANSFERABILITY

Despite its white middle-class American origins, it is applicable in a wide variety of situations (business, education, marriage, individual therapy, rehabilitation, etc.) and seems to make sense to people of varying cultural backgrounds. TA has spread not only into Western Europe, but also has many practitioners in Australia, Japan, India and South America, for example.

COMPLEMENTARY NATURE

In its organisational application, it integrates, complements and verifies other approaches to organisational and managerial behaviour (see Chapter 15).

AUTHORITY

As a model, it is very helpful in helping people to deal with authority issues, particularly through the concepts of Parent and Adapted Child. It certainly helps those low in personal power to assert without being aggressive and to take care of themselves and prevent or limit exploitation.

WORK AND NON-WORK

It can be used in non-work as well as work situations. At first sight, this may seem a disadvantage. However, no effective model of human relationships or approach to interpersonal skills training is likely to be self-restricting to the purely organisational aspects of life. TA concepts such as 'stamps' underline the futility of attempting to separate organisational and non-organisational behaviour, much as some people in organisations would like this to be possible (the 'don't bring your personal problems to work' syndrome). Whilst personal therapy is not the aim of TA training at work, many participants do have quasi-therapeutic experiences on TA courses and there have been examples of people giving up sedatives or anti-depressants after TA-based training.

OPTIMISTIC

Above all, TA is an optimistic theory of behaviour in that it affirms our capacity to change and become more effective in our dealings with others despite our past history and current circumstances, including the constraints on our working situation. In fact it seems likely that in future TA may have a greater impact on our organisational, social and cultural systems than at the purely individual therapeutic level.

REFERENCES

1 P. Warr, M. Bird and N. Rackham, *Evaluation of Management Training*, Gower Press, 1970.
2 N. Rackham and T. Morgan, *Behaviour Analysis in Training*, McGraw-Hill, 1977. (This book contains useful material on the evaluation of interpersonal skills training.)
3 C.L. Cooper and D. Bowles, 'Hurt or helped', *Training Information Paper* no. 10, Training Services Agency, 1977.
4 L.K. Randall, 'Red, white and blue TA at 600 mph' in *Everybody Wins: TA Applied to Organisations*', D. Jongeward et al., Addison-Wesley, 1973.
5 T. Kilcourse, 'TA under attack' in *Personnel Management*, June 1978.
6 F. Capra, *The Tao of Physics*, Wildwood House, 1975.
7 M. Groder, 'Groder's 5 OK diagrams' in *TA After Eric Berne*, Graham Barnes (ed), Harper's College Press, 1977.
8 K.D. Benne, 'The processes of re-education: An assessment of Kurt Lewin's views' in *Group and Organisation Studies* vol. 1, no. 1, J.E. Jones and J.W. Pfeiffer (eds), University Associates Inc., 1976.
9 C. Naranjo, *The One Quest*, Wildwood House, 1972.

Appendix 1 A TA booklist

MANAGEMENT AND ORGANISATIONAL

Berne, Eric, *The Structure and Dynamics of Organisations and Groups*, J.B. Lippincott Co., 1963; Grove Press Inc., 1975.
An outline of Berne's frameworks for examining group and organisational processes.

Carby, K., and Thakur, M., *TA at Work*, Institute of Personnel Management, 1976.
Introduction to TA theory, its application to organisations and a review of its use in some British organisations.

James, M., *The OK Boss*, Addison-Wesley, 1975.
Review of management style and behaviour in TA terms.

Jongeward, D., and James, M., *Winning with People: Group Exercises in Transactional Analysis*, Addison-Wesley, 1973.
A book on the basics of TA theory with many individual and group exercises, suitable for trainers and managers.

Jongeward, D., et al., *Everybody Wins: Transactional Analysis Applied to Organisations*, Addison-Wesley 1973.
The first book to present the use of TA in organisations. Includes some material relating TA to established theories of management and organisations.

Morrison, J.H., and O'Hearne, J.J., *Practical Transactional Analysis in Management*, Addison-Wesley, 1977.
An analysis of the uses of TA for improving the effectiveness of managers and organisations.

Novey, T.B., *TA for Management*, Jalmar Press Inc., 1976.
In-depth consideration of the application of TA for management and managers.

GENERAL AND THERAPY

Barnes, G. (ed), *TA After Eric Berne: Teachings and Practice of three TA Schools*, Harper's College Press, 1977.
Up-to-date view of the theory, practices, applications and philosophies of TA.

Berne, Eric, *Transactional Analysis in Psychotherapy*, Grove Press Inc., 1961; Souvenir Press, 1975.
The first description by Berne of the principles involved in the TA approach to therapy.

Berne, Eric, *Games People Play: The Psychology of Human Relation-*

ships, Grove Press Inc., 1964; Penguin Books, 1968.
Berne's best-seller that first introduced TA to the public at large.

Berne, Eric, *Principles of Group Treatment*, Grove Press Inc., 1966.
A review of the practices and procedures of group therapy, including the use of TA.

Berne, Eric, *Sex in Human Loving*, Simon and Schuster, 1970; Penguin Books, 1973.
A TA view of male–female relationships.

Berne, Eric, *What do you say after you say Hello? – The Psychology of Human Destiny*, Grove Press Inc., 1972; Corgi, 1975.
Berne's last book before he died, detailing his view of scripts.

Harris, T.A., *I'm OK – You're OK*, Harper and Row, 1969; Pan Books, 1973.
A general over-view of TA and its implications for some wider aspects of society and human existence.

James, M., and Jongeward, D., *Born to Win; Transactional Analysis with Gestalt Experiments*, Addison-Wesley, 1971.
A book for the layman, reviewing TA theory and its application in everyday life, together with some Gestalt exercises.

James, M., et al., *Techniques in Transactional Analysis for Psychotherapists and Counsellors*, Addison-Wesley, 1977.
A recent book on the theory, practice, applications and philosophy of TA, with a section comparing it with other therapies.

Levin, P., *Becoming the Way We Are: A Transactional Guide to Personal Development*, Group House, 1974.
A book describing child and adolescent development in TA terms.

Schiff, J.L., et al., *Cathexis Reader; Transactional Analysis Treatment of Psychosis*, Harper and Row, 1975.
A book describing the 'cathexis' approach to the TA-based treatment of psychotic illnesses.

Steiner, C.M., *Games Alcoholics Play*, Grove Press Inc., 1971.
The use of TA in the analysis and treatment of alcoholism.

Steiner, C.M., *Scripts People Live: Transactional Analysis of Life Scripts*, Grove Press Inc., 1974; Bantam Books, 1975.
A detailed analysis of script theory, including male and female scripts, therapy related to scripts, the idea of TA contracts and a 'mini-biography' of Berne (including Berne's own script).

Woollams, S., and Brown, M., *Transactional Analysis; A Modern and Comprehensive Text of TA Theory and Practice*, Huron Valley Institute Press, 1978.
A recent book reviewing TA theory and practice.

Woollams, S., Brown, M., and Huige, K., *Transactional Analysis in Brief*, Huron Valley Institute, 1974.
A brief outline of the main theory areas of TA.

Appendix 2 Useful addresses

International Transactional Analysis Association
1772 Vallejo Street
San Francisco
California 94123
United States of America

Institute of Transactional Analysis
The Secretary
Abbey Mews
Calder Abbey
Calderbridge
West Cumbria

Group Relations Training Association
Hon. Secretary
Guy Wareing
Gulf Oil
The Quadrangle
Imperial Square
Cheltenham
Gloucester

Association for Humanistic Psychology in Britain
62 Southwark Bridge Road
London SE1 0AS

London Gestalt Centre
5 Wrentham Avenue
London NW10

British Association for Counselling
1a Little Church Street
Rugby
Warwickshire CV21 3AP

OD Network
ODN Secretariat
Latchetts
Butchers Lane
Preston
Hitchin
Hertford SG4 7TR

Index